The Steve Jobs Story

Tom Christian

Level 4
(2000-word)

IBC パブリッシング

はじめに

　ラダーシリーズは、「はしご (ladder)」を使って一歩一歩上を目指すように、学習者の実力に合わせ、無理なくステップアップできるよう開発された英文リーダーのシリーズです。

　リーディング力をつけるためには、繰り返したくさん読むこと、いわゆる「多読」がもっとも効果的な学習法であると言われています。多読では、「1. 速く 2. 訳さず英語のまま 3. なるべく辞書を使わず」に読むことが大切です。スピードを計るなど、速く読むよう心がけましょう（たとえば TOEIC® テストの音声スピードはおよそ1分間に150語です）。そして1語ずつ訳すのではなく、英語を英語のまま理解するくせをつけるようにします。こうして読み続けるうちに語感がついてきて、だんだんと英語が理解できるようになるのです。まずは、ラダーシリーズの中からあなたのレベルに合った本を選び、少しずつ英文に慣れ親しんでください。たくさんの本を手にとるうちに、英文書がすらすら読めるようになってくるはずです。

《本シリーズの特徴》
- 中学校レベルから中級者レベルまで5段階に分かれています。自分に合ったレベルからスタートしてください。
- クラシックから現代文学、ノンフィクション、ビジネスと幅広いジャンルを扱っています。あなたの興味に合わせてタイトルを選べます。
- 巻末のワードリストで、いつでもどこでも単語の意味を確認できます。レベル1、2では、文中の全ての単語が、レベル3以上は中学校レベル外の単語が掲載されています。
- カバーにヘッドホーンマークのついているタイトルは、オーディオ・サポートがあります。ウェブから購入/ダウンロードし、リスニング教材としても併用できます。

《使用語彙について》
レベル1:中学校で学習する単語約1000語
レベル2:レベル1の単語+使用頻度の高い単語約300語
レベル3:レベル1の単語+使用頻度の高い単語約600語
レベル4:レベル1の単語+使用頻度の高い単語約1000語
レベル5:語彙制限なし

Contents

Foreword 3

Part 1 California dreaming 7

Part 2 An entrepreneur is born 23

Part 3 Time out 41

Part 4 The return of the king 55

Word List 90

読み始める前に

【読み進める上で知っておくと役に立つ単語】

- A player
- arrogant
- Big Brother
- bozo
- digital hub
- interim
- minimalist
- multi-touch
- prank
- see-through
- shit
- sugared water

【ジョブズの家族】

Abdulfattah Jandali アブドゥルファター・ジャンダーリ 実の父親。シリア出身のイスラム教徒。

Joanne Schieble ジョアン・シーブル ウィスコンシン州の田舎、ドイツ系移民の家庭で生まれる。実の母親。

Paul Jobs ポール・ジョブズ 養父。ローンを払えなくなった車の回収業で生計をたてる。

Clara Jobs クララ・ジョブズ 養母。会計事務の仕事をしていた。

Stephen Wozniak スティーブ・ウォズニアック 同じ高校の卒業生で、アップル・コンピュータ社の共同創設者の1人。

Chrisann Brenna クリスアン・ブレナン 最初のガールフレンド。1978年には娘のLisa (リサ) を生むが結婚はしなかった。

Mona Simpson モナ・シンプソン 実の妹。ニューヨークで小説家として才能を発揮する。

Laurene Powell ローレン・パウエル 妻。スティーブとの間にリード、エリン、イブの3人の子供をもうける。

【スティーブ・ジョブズの生涯とアップル社の変遷】

1955年 2月24日、サンフランシスコで生まれ、すぐにジョブズ家に養子に出される。

1968年 13才になるとクリスチャンになることを拒否し、インドや日本などに興味を持ち始める。

1971年 ウォズニアックとともにブルーボックスを作る。

1972年　オレゴン州のリード・カレッジへ進学するもすぐに退学し、好きな授業だけを無断で受けていた。

1974年　2月には大学を離れ、アタリ社での仕事を得る。

1977年　1月、アップル・コンピュータ社をウォズニアックと共に設立。

1977年　Apple IIを発表。その後16年間で600万台が生産された。

1978年　5月に娘(リサ)が生まれる。

1979年　Apple IIを打ち破るべく、Lisaプロジェクトが始まる。12月にはXeroxがアップルに100万ドルの投資を決定。そのころ、ジョブズはLisaプロジェクトから外される。

1980年　アップル社、ニューヨーク市場に上場し、時価総額は2.5億ドル。

1983年　ペプシから新社長を迎える。

1984年　1月にMacintoshを発表。その後売り上げは伸び悩んだ。

1985年　3月時点で売上目標の10%しか達成できず、ついにジョブズはMacintosh部門を外される。2ヶ月後、取締役の決定を受け、ジョブズは1株を残し全株を売却し、Appleを解任され、NeXT社を設立。

1986年　資金ショートをきたしたNeXT社にロス・ペローが投資。ルーカスフィルム社を買収し、Pixarとして独立会社を設立した。

1989年　スタンフォード大学のスピーチ会場でローレンと出会う。

1991年　ローレンと結婚。

1996年　OS開発が行き詰まっていたApple社が、NeXT社を買収。これにより、ジョブズはApple社に戻る(1997年)。

1998年　iMacを市場に投入。

2001年　アップル・ストア1号店をオープンさせる。日本で大容量のハードドライブを見て、iPodを思いつく。

2003年 iTunesストアをオープンする。その後、iPod mini、shuffle、nanoを市場に投入。この頃、膵臓に癌が見つかる。

2005年 スタンフォード大学の卒業式で、スピーチをする。iPhoneの前身となるROKRを発表。

2007年 iPhoneを開発、販売を開始。

2009年 肝臓移植手術を受ける。術後、仕事に復帰。

2010年 iPadを発表する。

2011年 1月に休職を発表、8月にはCEOとしてティム・クックを指名。10月5日、パロアルトの自宅で死去。享年56歳。

cover photo: Apple Computer launches online music distribution service in Japan
Apple Computer Inc. Chief Executive Officer Steve Jobs said Aug. 4 in Tokyo that his company has launched an online music distribution service in Japan in collaboration with 15 Japanese music companies including Avex Inc. (Photo: Kyodo News)

The Steve Jobs Story

Tom Christian

Foreword

Not a normal businessman

Steve Jobs, one of the two founders of the computer company Apple, died from cancer on October 5, 2011. He was only fifty-six years old.

In the days after his death, people gathered at Apple Stores around the world to remember him. They placed messages and flowers and candles outside the shops. More than a million people e-mailed messages to a website Apple set up in his memory. Millions of people talked about him on Facebook and Twitter.

The president of the United States and the prime minister of Great Britain commented on Jobs's death. The media said that the last time the public were so sad was the death of Michael Jackson in 2009 or the death of Princess Diana in a car crash in 1997.

But Steve Jobs wasn't a pop star or a princess. He was a businessman; but he was certainly no ordinary businessman.

Jobs pioneered the personal computer revolution in the 1970s. Although he was a millionaire at the age of twenty-five, he had to leave his own company in 1985, when he was thirty. In 1997, twelve years later, Apple was in trouble. Jobs went back and built Apple into one of the most valuable companies in the world. Stylish products like the iPod, iPhone, and iPad are now part of the everyday life of millions of people everywhere.

Why did people admire Steve Jobs so much? Perhaps it was because of his passion. He didn't care about money. He just wanted to make great products. "Being the richest man in the cemetery doesn't matter," he once said. "Doing something wonderful . . . that's what matters to me."

This is his story.

Flowers in memory of Apple co-founder Steve Jobs are seen outside an Apple Store.

Photo: Kyodo News

Part 1

California dreaming

Adoption and early life

Steve Jobs was born on February 24, 1955. His father was Abdulfattah Jandali, a Syrian teaching assistant at the University of Wisconsin. His mother was Joanne Schieble, a graduate student at the same university.

During a visit to Jandali's home in Syria in the summer of 1954, Joanne had gotten pregnant. Her father did not want her to marry a Muslim, so the young couple had to put their baby boy up for adoption.

Joanne believed that education was important. For that reason, she wanted her baby to be adopted by college graduates. But it didn't happen that way. The graduate couple who were scheduled to adopt her baby wanted a girl. They were not interested in a boy.

So, in their place, Paul and Clara Jobs of San Francisco, California adopted Joanne's baby boy. Neither Paul nor Clara had been to college. Paul worked as a "repo man" (getting back cars from people who could not repay their car loans), and Clara was a bookkeeper. Still, they promised they would save up money to send Steve to college.

Paul and Clara had been married for nine years but had not been able to have a baby. They were very happy with their new baby and called him Steven Paul Jobs. They later adopted another child, a girl called Patty.

Lessons in craftsmanship

Paul Jobs had not gone to university, but he loved machines, especially cars. In fact, he saved up the money to send Steve to college by buying broken-down cars and repairing them. He gave Steve some space on his workbench in the garage so they could work on things together.

Paul taught young Steve the importance of making things properly. A real craftsman was careful about every part of the things he made, Paul said. That included the parts no one saw, like the back of a fence or a cupboard. That's why Steve later cared so much about the design inside Apple products.

Steve also learned about good design from the house where his family lived. An architect called Joseph Eichler had built it. Eichler wanted to make well-designed homes for ordinary Americans. Living in the Eichler house inspired Steve to create simple, nicely designed products for ordinary people when he was at Apple.

Engineering hotspot

The Jobs family lived in the San Francisco Bay Area. Lots of companies that produced things for the military, such as Lockheed and Westinghouse, were based there. There were also new technology companies like Hewlett-Packard and, from the 1960s, semiconductor firms like Fairchild and Intel. As a result, many of the fathers in the Jobs family's neighborhood were engineers. Jobs grew up admiring people who knew about science and technology.

At elementary school, Steve was bored, and so he behaved badly. Then in fourth grade, he got a good teacher called Imogene Hill. She saw Steve was special and arranged for him to skip a grade.

When Steve was thirteen, he decided that he did not want to be a Christian. If God knew everything, why wasn't He helping the people who were dying from hunger in Africa? That was when Steve started to become very interested in religions from other countries like India and Japan.

As Steve got older, he also became more and more interested in electronics. When he was fifteen, he put speakers around his family's house so he could listen to what was happening in other rooms. His father was not happy about that!

Steve also joined the Hewlett-Packard Explorers Club. This was a group of students who met in the company cafeteria once a week to listen to an HP engineer talk about his work.

It was at the Explorers Club that Steve first saw a computer. He also got the idea of building a machine called a frequency counter. In the phone book, he found the phone number of Bill Hewlett, one of the founders of HP, and called him. They spoke for 20 minutes. Hewlett didn't just give Steve some components for the machine for free, he also gave him a job in the HP factory. Steve was always a good talker!

In his last year at high school, Steve started experimenting with drugs like LSD and marijuana, listening to more music, and reading books that were not connected to science or technology. Later he said that doing things like this helped him think differently from other people—and design better products than they could, too.

It was at this time that Steve Jobs met Stephen Wozniak, with whom he later founded Apple Computer.

Stephen Wozniak

Wozniak was five years older than Jobs. Unlike Jobs, Wozniak was very shy. His father, who was a rocket scientist at Lockheed, had taught him about electronics from a very young age.

Electronics was a game for Wozniak. As a child, he had built an intercom system for the boys in his neighborhood. He regularly won prizes for devices he had built himself.

As a teenager, Wozniak became fascinated with computers. He read his father's computer magazines and tried to redesign the computers with as few parts as possible. (He didn't have enough money to actually buy the parts and build computers, so he just drew the plans.)

Wozniak dropped out of college after two years and started building a computer in a friend's garage. That friend was called Bill Fernandez. It was Fernandez who introduced Jobs and Wozniak.

Apple CEO Steve Jobs stands in front of a photo of himself, right, and Steve Wozniak, left, during an Apple event in San Francisco.

Photo: AP Photo / Paul Sakuma

The two young men were very similar—and very different. They both loved electronics, the music of Bob Dylan, and playing pranks, but Wozniak was shy and timid, while Jobs was outgoing and self-confident. It was the balance in their personalities that made them such an effective pair.

Making the Blue Box

In September 1971, Wozniak read a story about people called "phone phreakers" in a magazine. Phone phreakers were like hackers today. The phreakers had developed a trick to use sound to control telephones and make long-distance phone calls without paying. To do this, they used a machine called a "Blue Box."

Jobs and Wozniak were very interested. They built their own Blue Box and started making free calls with it. They even called the Vatican in Rome. Wozniak put on a

German accent and pretended to be Henry Kissinger, U.S. secretary of state. "Ve are at de summit meeting in Moscow, and ve need to talk to de pope," he said.

Blue Box at the Computer History Museum

Then Jobs had an idea. Why didn't they build and sell Blue Boxes as a business? It only cost $40 to buy the parts, and they could sell the machines for $150 each. A nice profit! They built around one hundred machines and sold them to college students all over California.

This was the first time Jobs and Wozniak had worked together. Wozniak took care of the technical side of things, and Jobs was the "ideas man" in charge of vision, getting parts, and making sales. The two young men were breaking the law, but the experience gave them confidence in what they could do together.

Going to college

Steve Jobs never believed in doing the easy thing. He lived close to two top universities, Berkeley and Stanford, but told his parents he wanted to go to Reed College in Oregon. Reed was a small liberal arts school. It had high academic standards but was very expensive.

In the early 1970s, the hippie culture was very strong. Jobs and his friends at Reed were typical hippies, interested in Zen Buddhism, meditation, vegetarianism, and drugs.

One person who influenced Jobs at Reed was Robert Friedland. Friedland had set up a commune in a nearby apple orchard. Friedland had extraordinary charisma. He was able to control people by the force of his personality. This was a technique Jobs copied and used later at Apple.

Jobs quickly got bored at Reed and dropped out of regular courses. He started attending courses that interested him, even though he wasn't paying fees anymore!

One of the classes he attended was about calligraphy. There Jobs learned all about different fonts. This knowledge was very important later when Jobs created personal computers. Apple computers were the first in the world to offer users a variety of fonts, and Apple is still the favorite computer of designers today.

Jobs enjoyed this life, but it wasn't easy. He lived in a garage for $20 a month. Every Sunday, he walked to the nearby Hare Krishna temple for a free vegetarian meal. He also earned a little money by returning bottles to stores to get the deposit.

First job at Atari

In February 1974, Jobs left Reed and went home to California to look for a job. His approach was unusual. He walked into the lobby of Atari, the first-ever video game company, and said he would not leave until Atari gave him a job!

Nolan Bushnell, the founder of the company, liked Jobs's crazy attitude and offered him a job. There was one problem, however. No one else at the company wanted to work with Jobs. Jobs believed that because he ate only fruits and vegetables, he would not sweat or smell bad, even if he never took a bath. Sadly, this was not true. He never bathed—and he smelled terrible!

In the end, Atari asked Jobs to work at night when there were no other workers nearby. But Jobs didn't stay long at the company. He wanted to go to India to "find enlightenment." Jobs did some work for Atari in Germany and Italy, so they paid for his ticket to Europe. He then got another ticket for the rest of the way.

Jobs spent about seven months in India. A lot of the time he was sick. When he got back to California, his hair was shaved and his skin was dark. He again joined Atari.

At the time, Atari's best-selling video game was called Pong. Just like ping-pong, two people hit a ball to one another using paddles. The boss of Atari wanted to create a one-player version of the game, and he asked Jobs to design it.

Jobs contacted Wozniak and asked him to make the game. Wozniak, who was working designing calculators at Hewlett-Packard, designed it in just four days using very few chips. Jobs built the prototype.

Once again, Jobs and Wozniak had shown how well they worked together.

The Homebrew Computer Club

In March 1975, a new club called the Homebrew Computer Club was set up. It was for people who built their own computers and TVs as a hobby.

Wozniak was a member of the club. One

day, he read a description of a microprocessor there. This gave him the idea of creating a desktop personal computer. He started building his computer in the evenings at Hewlett-Packard.

The computer was ready to test on June 29, 1975. Wozniak typed a few keys, and letters came up on the screen for the first time in history.

Wozniak was good-natured and not very business-minded. He wanted to give the plans of his personal computer to the other members of the club for free. Jobs had a different idea. Why didn't they build the computers and sell them?

Part 2

An entrepreneur is born

Setting up Apple

The two friends decided to start their own company. Jobs sold his Volkswagen bus, and Wozniak sold his calculator. They had $1,300. Now they needed a name for their company.

They chose "Apple" because it started with an A, because it was simple and friendly, and because Jobs liked eating fruit and vegetables.

Originally, the company had three founders: Jobs, Wozniak, and Ron Wayne, who worked at Atari. But Wayne was afraid of the risk and soon dropped out.

The boss of a small local chain of specialized computer shops saw Wozniak and Jobs present their computer at the Homebrew Computer Club. He was impressed and gave

Jobs his business card. The next day, Jobs walked barefoot into one of the man's stores and persuaded him to buy fifty computers for $500 each.

Apple Computer had got its first order for $25,000! Jobs and his friends and family got started building their first computer, the Apple I, in the Jobs family's garage. These first computers were very simple. They did not include a power supply, a case, a keyboard, or a monitor. That meant that only computer fans could use them.

Apple I, Apple's first product, at the Smithsonian Museum

A new partner

Jobs soon realized that the hobbyists like him and Wozniak who enjoyed building their own computers were not the biggest market. No, the really big market was ordinary people who wanted a computer that was ready to use out of the box.

Building a complete consumer product like that was going to cost money. Jobs needed to find an investor. Through his connections at Atari, Jobs was introduced to Mike Markkula.

Markkula had worked at the two first semiconductor companies, Fairchild and Intel. He had made so much money from his stock in Intel that he had already retired, even though he was only in his thirties.

Markkula was impressed with Jobs. The two men wrote a business plan together. They imagined an age when every family would have its own personal computer.

Markkula was very positive. "We will be a Fortune 500 company in two years," he said. "This is the start of a new industry."

Originally, Jobs and Wozniak had held 50% of the company each. After Markkula invested $250,000, he, Jobs, and Wozniak had about one-third each. Wozniak, who was still working at Hewlett-Packard, finally gave up his job to focus full-time on Apple.

A unique philosophy and image

The new company, Apple Computer Co., was created on January 3, 1977. Markkula was like a mentor to Jobs. He wrote a marketing philosophy for Apple. The important thing was not to make money, Markkula believed. What they wanted was to build a company that would last for a long time.

The Apple philosophy was based on three key ideas.

1. **Empathy**—Apple was going to connect with the customers' feelings.
2. **Focus**—Apple was going to concentrate only on what was important.
3. **Impute**—People judge things by their appearance. Apple packaging and products therefore needed to look good.

To help create a professional image for Apple, Jobs contacted Regis McKenna, a famous Silicon Valley publicist. McKenna created the famous logo of an apple with a bite taken out of it for them. He also made a slogan for the company: "Simplicity is the ultimate sophistication."

Jobs himself was not very sophisticated. He was aggressive, smelly, and seldom wore shoes.

In April 1977, at the West Coast Computer Faire, Apple introduced its consumer computer.

Apple II with Disk II floppy disk drives

The Apple II included VisiCalc (a spreadsheet software similar to Excel). It was a smash hit. Over 16 years, nearly six million units were sold.

Lisa: a daughter and a computer

In May 1978, Jobs's then-girlfriend Chrisann Brennan gave birth to a baby girl, Lisa. Jobs did not want to marry Chrisann. In fact, he did not even give her and the baby any money until the County used a DNA test to prove he was the father. After that, he had to support her.

Wozniak had created the Apple II. Now Jobs wanted to create his own computer. He assembled a team of engineers and started work on a new model. He called it…the Lisa. Many people thought it was strange that he gave the computer the same name as the daughter he was not looking after.

While Jobs was working on the Lisa, he

had an experience that changed the history of personal computers. In December 1979, Xerox, the photocopier company, invested $1 million in Apple. In return for being allowed to invest, Xerox let Jobs visit the Xerox Palo Alto Research Center (Xerox PARC).

At Xerox PARC, Jobs saw a computer with a graphical user interface (GUI) for the first time. A graphical user interface meant that the screen of the computer showed a desktop with documents and folders. Everything was controlled with a mouse.

GUI computers were so easy that ordinary, non-technical people could understand and use them. Jobs was very excited by what he saw at Xerox PARC. He felt that this was the future of computing. He decided that Apple would make GUI computers, too.

Inside Apple, however, things were not going smoothly. The engineers on the Lisa project did not like Jobs's rudeness and aggression and the way he always wanted to change things. So many people complained that, in the end, he was removed from the Lisa project.

The birth of the Macintosh

In December 1980, Apple's shares were listed on the New York stock market. Although Jobs was only 25 years old, his stock was worth over $250 million. Handsome young Steve Jobs became the symbol of a new breed of Silicon Valley entrepreneur.

Jef Raskin, an engineer at Apple, was in charge of a project called Macintosh. His plan was to create a cheap $1,000 computer for ordinary people.

After losing the Lisa project, Jobs was looking for something to do. He pushed Raskin out and took over the Macintosh project. He increased the number of engineers on the team. Jobs didn't care if the computer was cheap or profitable. He wanted it to be "great."

First of all, he wanted it to be small. The bottom of the computer should be no bigger than a telephone book, he told his staff. Because he wanted the text display to be attractive, he got a high school friend to develop all sorts of new fonts for the computer.

Jobs also wanted the Macintosh to have an attractive case. To find a good designer, he organized a design contest. The winner was Hartmut Esslinger, a German who had designed Sony's Trinitron televisions.

Jobs liked German design. He loved Porsche and Mercedes cars, and he was a big

Apple Lisa, with an Apple Pro File external hard drive stacked on top of it

fan of Dieter Rams (b. 1932), the German industrial designer who designed electronic devices for Braun. Jobs, like Rams, believed that simple, easy-to-understand design was best. For the Macintosh, Jobs wanted Esslinger to create a white, "high-tech" look, the opposite of the heavy, black, "industrial" look of Sony.

A new president from Pepsi

Apple was growing fast. It had sold 2,500 computers in 1977, but it sold 210,000 in 1981. The company was quite chaotic, though. For example, the three models it was making or developing, the Apple II, the Macintosh, and Lisa, all used different software. The Macintosh was very behind schedule. Jobs had such a strong personality that he was difficult to control. And competition was increasing. IBM introduced its personal computer to the market in August 1981.

Mike Markkula decided it was time to look for a new president to lead the fast-growing company. The man they chose was John Sculley. Sculley was president of the Pepsi-Cola division of PepsiCo. He had successfully increased sales of Pepsi with a series of advertisements called the "Pepsi Challenge." Sculley was thought to be a marketing genius.

Sculley's background, however, was very different from that of Jobs. His father was a New York lawyer, while Jobs' father was a mechanic. Sculley was a "company man" who had worked at Pepsi all his life, while Jobs had worked nights at Atari for only a few months before setting up his own company.

But Apple—and Steve Jobs—wanted Sculley. They liked the way he had sold Pepsi not as a drink, but as a "lifestyle choice" for young people. They wanted him to do the same thing for their computers.

Jobs worked hard to persuade Sculley to

join Apple. He met him several times and agreed to pay him a $1 million salary and a $1 million bonus for taking the job.

One day in New York, Jobs looked Sculley in the eye and asked him, "Do you want to spend the rest of your life selling sugared water, or do you want a chance to change the world?" Sculley was so shocked he couldn't breathe. That was when he finally said yes.

Culture shock

John Sculley flew to California in May 1983. It was a big culture shock. He was used to the East Coast style of doing business: men in suits and formal manners. Apple meetings, with lots of young people in jeans shouting at one another, were a big surprise.

At first, Jobs and Sculley got on well, but gradually Jobs began to feel that Sculley was not the right man for the job. Sculley promoted the wrong people, and did not love the products the way Steve did. He was not a "product guy;" he just wanted to get rich.

One big argument Jobs and Sculley had was about the price of the Macintosh computer. The original plan was to sell it for $1,000, but Jobs had made so many changes that such a low price was impossible. Jobs wanted to sell it for $1,995, but Sculley said that because of marketing costs, they would have to sell it for $2,495. Sculley was the president, and he won the fight.

The launch of the Macintosh

Jobs wanted to launch the Macintosh in a dramatic way. By 1983, IBM personal computers were the best-selling computers in the market. IBM was an old, large, and traditional company. Jobs therefore wanted to make an advertisement in which "cool" little Apple fought back against big, corporate, "boring" IBM.

An entrepreneur is born

The Mac was going to be launched in January 1984. Because everyone associated the year 1984 with George Orwell's book *1984* about a totalitarian state, Jobs decided to make that the theme of the advertisement.

Apple hired Ridley Scott, the director of *Blade Runner*. He made a commercial in which a woman runs through a crowd and throws a hammer into a screen with a picture of Big Brother. The message was clear: "Don't let IBM control the world. Get

Steve Jobs announcing the Apple Macintosh computer on January 24, 1984 in California

Photo: Kyodo News

an Apple Mac and be a cool young rebel."

The commercial was shown during the Super Bowl on January 22, 1984. Nearly 100 million people watched it. It was a sensation.

On January 24, Jobs launched the Macintosh at an event in California. It featured music, graphics, spreadsheets—and it could even talk!

The success of the Macintosh made Jobs even more arrogant than before. He was put in charge of the Lisa division, as well as the Macintosh division. He fired a lot of the Lisa people, told the rest of them they were no good, and put "his" people from the Macintosh division into the top jobs.

He also decided to build a factory to make the Macintosh. He wanted the factory to be beautiful, so he painted all the equipment in bright colors. But as it was delicate, the equipment stopped working properly when it was painted. This was typical of how Jobs would put design above simple common sense.

An entrepreneur is born

Jobs was not an easy man to work for. He thought he was special. He thought he didn't have to follow the rules like normal people. Other people took care to be polite, but he said exactly what he thought, even if he was rude and hurt people.

He also had an extreme way of looking at things. People were either "geniuses" or "idiots," "heroes" or "bozos." Their work was "great," or it was "shit." Some people found Jobs's criticism inspiring. It made them work harder, and they achieved amazing things. Other people could not bear it.

Arrogant and difficult people get a lot of enemies. If you have a lot of enemies, you need to be successful, or your enemies will attack you. Sadly for Jobs, the Apple Mac, after an impressive start, was not selling very well. In March 1985, for example, it only sold 10% of its target.

With things going badly, Jobs just became even ruder and more aggressive. No one wanted to work with him, and managers started complaining to John Sculley about him. Sculley removed him from the Macintosh division.

Jobs now had nothing to do. Sculley suggested that Jobs became a "global visionary," but Jobs was a "product guy." He wanted real responsibility for developing real products.

Jobs took a holiday in Europe. When he came back to Apple, he announced that he was going to resign. In August 1985, he left the company and sold all his Apple stock (except one share).

Part 3

··●··

Time out

What's NeXT?

Jobs decided he was going to use his money—$100 million—to create a computer for the educational market. To do this, he set up a new company called NeXT with a few colleagues from Apple.

The first thing Jobs did was ask Paul Rand, one of the world's most famous designers, to create a logo for his new company. Normal designers make several designs for customers to choose from. Rand made just one design, and it cost $100,000.

Jobs spent too much money on other things, too. He bought a new furnished office and redesigned it completely. He also built a factory with beautiful white walls and colorful robots. He had decided to build a cube-shaped computer. The cube shape was very difficult and expensive for the engineers to build.

By late 1986, after one year in business, NeXT was already short of money. Luckily for Jobs, the Texas billionaire Ross Perot was eager to invest in the company. In 1979, Perot had missed a chance to invest in Microsoft. He didn't want to make the same mistake again, and he bought 16% of NeXT for $20 million.

Things inside NeXT were not going well, though. Jobs asked Bill Gates, his friend and rival, to make software for the machine. "What's the point in developing software for a computer that has no market?" Gates answered. IBM said they were interested in licensing NeXTSTEP (NeXT's operating system), but in the end, they chose not to.

On October 12, 1988, Jobs made a big presentation introducing the NeXT computer at the San Francisco Symphony Hall. The computer was very expensive, costing $6,500 without a printer or hard disk. And it was only going to come out in 1989.

When the NeXT computer came out, it sold very badly. The factory was able to make 10,000 computers a month, but they were only selling 400 a month. It was a disaster!

In the end, Jobs stopped making hardware and specialized in software. He sold the NeXT factory to the Japanese company Canon.

Meeting his mother and sister

In 1986, Jobs's mother Clara died from cancer. Soon after, with the help of a detective, he found out who his birth mother was. He also learned that she was living in Los Angeles.

After giving Jobs up for adoption, Joanne and Abdulfattah, Jobs's birth father, had got married. They had another child, a daughter called Mona. (Later, Abdulfattah had left Joanne, and she had married another man.)

Time out

Like her brother, Jobs's sister Mona was very talented. She was a novelist and lived in New York. After she and Jobs met, they became lifelong friends. In 1996, Mona wrote a novel called *A Regular Guy*. It was about a Silicon Valley millionaire and the daughter he had with a woman he was not married to. Really, the book was about Jobs and his daughter Lisa.

Mona managed to find their father Abdulfattah. He was living in California and worked in the restaurant business. When he met Mona, he told her that he had worked in a restaurant where many famous technology people ate. One of them was Steve Jobs, who "gave him big tips."

Abdulfattah didn't know that Jobs was his son, and Mona didn't tell him. Jobs did not want to meet his father. But Joanne and Mona often spent Christmas with Jobs, and Mona made a beautiful speech at Jobs's memorial service.

Buying Pixar

In 1985, Jobs met a man named Ed Catmull. Catmull worked in the computer division of Lucasfilm, the film effects company of George Lucas, the creator of *Star Wars*.

Lucas was getting divorced, so he needed money fast. When Jobs offered him $10 million for the computer division, Lucas said yes. The company had three lines of business. It made hardware like the $125,000 Pixar Image Computer; it made software for rendering 3-D graphics; and it also had a digital animation business.

One of the company's successful products was the Computer Animation Production

The entrance to Pixar's studio lot in Emeryville, California

System (CAPS) it developed with Disney. CAPS helped to automate and speed up the process of making artwork for animated films. It was used in the 1989 Disney film *The Little Mermaid*.

John Lasseter

Pixar was doing badly, and Jobs had to fire many of the staff. One area he always continued to invest in, however, was animation. Originally, Pixar only made short animated films to help promote its own computers. The man in charge of Pixar's digital animation department was John Lasseter.

In 1986, Lasseter produced a short animated film about a desk lamp for the annual computer graphic conference. It was so good that it was nominated for an Academy Award. Then in 1988, *Tin Toy*, Lasseter's film about the relationship of a toy and a baby, won the Academy Award for animated short film. This was the first time a computer-generated film had won.

Although Jobs had by now invested $50 million in the company, all three of Pixar's divisions were losing money. But the success of *Tin Toy* caught the eye of Michael Eisner and Jeffrey Katzenberg, the top managers at Disney. First, they tried to get Lasseter to come to Disney. When he refused, they started looking at ways that Disney and Pixar could work together to make movies.

In May 1991, Disney and Pixar made a deal to co-produce a film. Disney was a much bigger company, so the terms of the deal favored Disney. Disney would own the film and its characters, and it would pay Pixar just 12% of the revenues from the film.

Toy Story

Lasseter proposed a film called *Toy Story* to Disney. It was about an old toy, a cowboy called Woody, and a flashy new toy, a spaceman called Buzz Lightyear, and their relationship with Andy, the boy who owned them.

The problem was that as part of the deal, Disney had creative control. Katzenberg kept telling Lasseter to change the story. Woody became a more and more disagreeable person (rather like a Hollywood executive). Finally, when the film was about half-complete, everyone accepted it was no good. Lasseter took back control and made Woody into a wise and charming character again.

Lasseter knew best. When *Toy Story* was released in November 1995, it was a huge hit. It earned $362 million worldwide.

Jobs decided to take advantage of the film's success to list Pixar on the NASDAQ stock market the same month. Jobs had invested $50 million in Pixar. Now his shares were worth $1.2 billion! The IPO also meant that Jobs could negotiate a better deal with Disney. They agreed to a 50/50 split for financing and profit-sharing in the future.

Lessons and love

Steve Jobs learned a lot in the years he was away from Apple.

From NeXT, he learned that a computer company does not need to manufacture its own products. He also learned that well-designed products won't sell if they're too expensive. From Pixar, he learned that people love the combination of technology and entertainment. These lessons would be useful to Jobs in the future.

This was also the time when Jobs met his wife. He talked about these years in the speech he made to graduating students at Stanford University in 2005.

I didn't see it then, but it turned out that getting fired from Apple was the best thing that could have ever happened to me. The heaviness of being successful was replaced by the lightness of being a beginner again, less sure about everything. It freed me to enter one of the most creative periods of my life.

During the next five years, I started a company named NeXT, another company named Pixar, and fell in love with an amazing woman who would become my wife. Pixar went on to create the world's first computer-animated feature film, Toy Story, and is now the most successful animation studio in the world. In a remarkable turn of events, Apple bought NeXT, I returned to Apple, and the technology we developed at NeXT is at the heart of Apple's current renaissance. And Laurene and I have a wonderful family together.

I'm pretty sure none of this would have happened if I hadn't been fired from Apple.

Meeting Mrs. Jobs

Funnily enough, Jobs met his wife at Stanford University when he was invited to give speech at the university's business school in October 1989. Laurene Powell was a tall, beautiful blonde in her mid-twenties. Having worked for three years at an investment bank, she quit and enrolled at Stanford after a long holiday in Italy.

Since all the chairs were taken, Laurene was sitting in the reserved seats at the front. As a result, she was sitting next to Jobs before he went on stage. He liked her and invited her out to dinner that night.

On New Year's Day 1990, Jobs asked Laurene to marry him. She said yes, but for a year nothing happened. Then, in December 1990, they went to Hawaii together. Again, Jobs told her he wanted to marry her. More importantly, Laurene got pregnant.

Jobs was nervous about getting married. Should he marry Laurene or his previous girlfriend? Finally he married Laurene on March 18, 1991. Jobs was thirty-six; Laurene was twenty-seven.

The ceremony was held in The Ahwahnee,

a big stone hotel in Yosemite National Park in California. Jobs's Zen Buddhism teacher conducted the ceremony. When it was over, everyone had a piece of wedding cake (made without eggs or milk) and went out for a hike. A very healthy wedding indeed!

The married couple moved into an English-style house with a beautiful garden in Palo Alto. Laurene and Jobs had three children: a boy named Reed in 1991, then a girl named Erin in 1995, and another girl named Eve in 1998.

Falling Apple, rising Microsoft

From the early 1990s, Apple's market share had started falling. Computers running Microsoft Windows software were much more popular. Since 1985, Microsoft had been copying and refining the Graphical User Interface that Jobs had seen at Xerox PARC and then pioneered. After the launch of Windows 95 in 1995, Macintosh sales fell dramatically. By 1996, Apple's share of the market was only 4%.

John Sculley had left Apple in 1993. The current CEO was a man called Gil Amelio. Amelio knew that to fight back against Microsoft, Apple needed a new operating system (OS). Because the OS it had developed in-house was no good, it needed a partner. Amelio considered buying two companies. One was NeXT, and the other was Be Inc.

On December 10, 1996, the two CEOs presented their operating systems to Apple. Of course, Jobs made the better presentation! Amelio quickly bought NeXT Computer for $400 million. It was decided that Steve would come back to Apple as an advisor to the chairman. He started work at his old company in January 1997.

Part 4

··●··

The return of the king

Jobs is back

One of the first things Jobs did was to make a speech at the Macworld conference. He wanted to change things. "Apple has got to get the spark back," he said. "The Mac didn't progress much in ten years. Windows caught up, so we have to produce an OS that's even better."

Jobs started giving people from NeXT key jobs at Apple. But the company was doing very badly. Talented people were leaving, and the media suggested Apple might collapse.

Jobs was never good at being Number 2. Finally, on July 4, 1997, the Apple board decided to fire Gil Amelio and bring Steve Jobs back as a board member. For two months, Jobs had no job title. In September, he became "interim CEO" on a salary of $1 a

The return of the king

year!

In August 1997, there was another Macworld conference, this time in Boston. Jobs made another speech. He was going to change the company.

"There are a lot of great people at Apple, but they're doing the wrong things because the plan has been wrong," he said. "I've found people who can't wait to follow a good strategy, but they can't because there hasn't been one."

At the end of his speech, Jobs announced a deal with Apple's old rival Microsoft. Microsoft was going to invest $150 million in the company and start developing Word and Excel for Mac.

Mac fans were shocked that Apple was making a deal with Microsoft, but the deal helped to save the company.

A new advertising campaign

Jobs always believed in products as a whole. Everything—engineering, design, packaging, advertising—had to be perfect. He decided to launch a major advertising campaign to remind the world what was special about Apple.

In his speech at the Boston Macworld conference, Jobs had talked about Apple customers. "The people who buy Apple products think differently," he said. "They are the creative spirits in this world, and they're out to change the world. We make tools for these kinds of people."

The advertising was based on this "think different" idea. Other computer makers talked about boring things like processor speed or memory capacity, but Apple was the computer for special, creative people.

The campaign had black and white photographs of great people—John Lennon,

The return of the king

Gandhi, Bob Dylan—with the words THINK DIFFERENT underneath.

Now Jobs needed to restructure the company so it could produce great products again. The first thing he did was ask all the product teams to explain if the products they were making were really necessary.

Jobs realized that the company was making far too many products. He decided to stop making 70% of them, including the Newton, the handheld personal digital assistant. He also stopped making printers and servers. Of course, he had to fire lots of people—3,000 of them.

He then drew a very simple strategy diagram. It was a square divided into four blocks. In the future, the company would focus on just four areas: 1. A desktop computer for design professionals; 2. A portable computer for design professionals; 3. A desktop computer for ordinary consumers; 4. A portable computer for ordinary consumers.

Jobs was never an easy man to get along

with. When he returned to Apple, however, he was able to build a team of top managers who were tough, calm, and talented enough to work with him, despite his difficult character. Jobs believed that big companies started failing when they hired too many "B players" or "bozos." Jobs wanted only "A players" on his team.

The A Team: Jonathan Ive

One of the most important A players was Jonathan Ive, the young head of the company's design team.

Ive was British. His father was a silversmith who had taught him to enjoy making things with his hands. Ive had first used a Mac at design school. He said he felt a "connection" with it.

After leaving college, Ive helped set up a design agency called Tangerine in London. When Tangerine did a job for Apple, Apple liked Ive's work so much that the company hired him in 1992.

Ive became head of design at Apple in 1996, but he wasn't happy. There was too much focus on making money, and not enough focus on good design. He was planning to leave Apple, when one day Jobs came into the studio. The two men started talking. Like Jobs, Ive was a big fan of German design, especially Dieter Rams.

Jobs and Ive liked each other immediately. Jobs had been planning to hire a new design chief, but he changed his mind. Ive was the right man! Jobs and Ive agreed that unlike other companies where the engineers controlled product design, at Apple the designers should be in charge. They also agreed that design was not just about what a product looked like. Design was about how a product worked, about the whole customer experience.

The iMac

The original Bondi Blue iMac

The first product that Ive and Jobs created together was the iMac. The idea was to make a computer that looked "different." Most desktop computers were heavy, ugly, beige things. The iMac was shaped like an egg or gumdrop. It looked friendly and playful.

Jobs and Ive chose a see-through blue case for the iMac. These blue cases were not cheap, but they gave the computer a special

Steve Jobs announces new colors for iMacs during his keynote address at Macworld on January 5, 1990.

Photo: Kyodo News

charm. Even people who were afraid of technology would not be afraid of an iMac.

The iMac went on sale in August 1998, a year and a half after Jobs returned to Apple. It sold 800,000 units before the end of the year and was Apple's best-selling computer up to that time. "Thinking different" was working!

The A Team: Tim Cook

Another important member of Jobs's new management team was Tim Cook. Cook had worked at companies like Compaq and IBM before joining Apple. He was an expert in procurement and supply chain management. He was also a very hard worker who often sent e-mails at 4:30 in the morning. In contrast to Jobs, he was very quiet and calm.

Cook closed more than half of Apple's warehouses, cut the number of suppliers from 100 to 24, and outsourced all manufacturing. Apple became a much more profitable and efficient company.

The A Team: Ron Johnson

Jobs had noticed that the way computers were sold was changing. In the early days, they were sold in small specialist stores run by people who loved computers. Now most of them were sold in ugly "big box" stores on the edge of town. The clerks in these stores didn't know much about technology. They certainly could not tell you what was special about a Mac.

That was why Jobs hired Ron Johnson from Target, the second-largest retailing chain in the U.S. Together, Jobs and Johnson would change the way computers were sold. They talked about how to make the best store possible for Apple products. They decided they wanted to sell Macs in big shops in smart locations in the middle of town.

They also wanted the stores to look good with simple, minimalist design. Adding a "Genius Bar," where people could get advice on using their Apple products, was another new concept. Johnson got the idea from the concierge service at five-star hotels.

Building—and rebuilding—a prototype

Millard Drexler, CEO of The Gap clothing chain, also gave Jobs some good advice about designing a store. "Build a model store where you can test all sorts of layouts," he said. So, in 2000, Apple built a prototype store inside a warehouse near the head office. The team met there once a week for six months to refine the store's look.

In the beginning, the store was arranged by product lines with different sections for the different kinds of computers. But just when everyone thought the design was finished, Johnson woke up in the night with a new idea. Shouldn't they organize the store by themes like music, photos, or movies?

Jobs agreed with Johnson, and they reorganized the store layout at the last minute. People often said this was something special about Apple. Other companies were happy to do things that were just okay. Apple always wanted to be 100% perfect. That's why the company would often "rewind" and make last-minute changes to get everything just right.

The first Apple Store opened on May 19, 2001 in McLean, Virginia, a rich suburb of Washington, D.C. By the time Steve Jobs died in 2011, there were about 350 Apple Stores worldwide. The store on Fifth Avenue in New York City actually made more money

The first Apple store, Tysons Corner in Virginia

per square foot than any other shop in the world!

The Apple Stores generate only about 15% of Apple's sales. But with their stylish look—plate glass, brushed steel, plain wood, and titanium and glass staircases—and their great customer service, they act as a 3-D advertisement for the brand.

Digital hub strategy

Apple's computers were now selling well, so Jobs decided the time was right for a new strategy. He had a vision that the personal computer would become a "digital hub."

What does "digital hub" mean? Originally, people used computers for practical things like writing letters or doing accounts. But in the future, Jobs believed they would start using their computers to have fun and be creative. The movies people recorded with their video cameras, the photos they took, the songs they downloaded—everything would be on their computers.

In 1999, Apple started releasing software to help people manage their personal multimedia content. These were products like iMovie (to edit home video), iTunes (to manage music), and iPhoto (to touch up and store photos).

The birth of the iPod

iTunes made it easy to manage and listen to music on your computer at home, but what about in the car or in the gym?

The first iPod

There weren't any good portable MP3 music players available back then. They were difficult to use and held very few songs.

Jobs always loved music. His favorites were Bob Dylan, the Beatles, and the Rolling Stones. He wanted Apple to make a portable music player that was easy to use and could

THE RETURN OF THE KING

hold many songs.

Jobs often went to Japan to see the latest technologies Japanese companies were developing. In February 2001, on a visit to Toshiba, he was shown a very small 5-gigabyte hard drive. 5G was enough to hold 1,000 songs!

Jobs wanted the new music player to be in stores by Christmas 2001. That meant it had to be ready to present to the press by October. Everyone had to work hard because there was so little time.

To make the player easy to use, Apple invented the Click Wheel. The Click Wheel made it easy to scroll through long lists of songs. Jobs also insisted that it should be possible to do whatever you wanted with a maximum of three clicks.

Jonathan Ive, the designer, had his own ideas about how to make Apple's music player different and stylish. He wanted to make the whole thing white—not just the player, but the headphones, too.

Apple called the new machine an "iPod." When Jobs presented it to the public on October 23, 2001, he pulled it out of his pocket to show how small it was.

The iPod was small, but at $399, it wasn't cheap. Still, it became a big hit, in part because of a great advertising campaign. Black silhouettes danced against colorful backgrounds while holding a white iPod with white wires that went up to their ears. The tagline was "1,000 songs in your pocket."

Once again, Jobs had found success by integrating hardware and software, technology and entertainment.

The iTunes Store

As a music lover, Jobs was worried about piracy. With people downloading music from the Internet, musicians were not getting paid for their work anymore.

THE RETURN OF THE KING

The record companies had tried to solve the problem by setting up online music stores like PressPlay (Sony and Universal) and MusicNet (Warner, EMI, Bertelsmann). But they were not very good services because they offered too few songs and didn't allow people to keep them.

Jobs thought that people didn't *want* to steal music but just couldn't get it any other way. He believed that people would buy music if he made the process easy. Jobs created the online iTunes Store to help people get the music they wanted and to pay the musicians who had created that music.

To make sure that the iTunes Store would offer a large number of songs, Jobs made deals with most of the big record companies. Because Apple only had 5% of the computer market in those days, the record companies did not think the company would become a big competitor.

When the iTunes store was introduced on April 28, 2003, it had 200,000 songs on offer. The songs were sold for 99 cents each.

Within one week, Apple sold six million songs. The iTunes Store went on to sell 1 billion songs by February 2006, 10 billion by February 2010, and 15 billion by June 2011! Apple is now the world's No. 1 music retailer.

Music takes off

Apple started introducing new models of the iPod. Small, lightweight models like the Mini (January 2004), Shuffle (January 2005), and Nano (September 2005) were very popular with joggers and gym users and pushed Apple's market share to above 70%.

Musicians were also interested in the iPod as a marketing tool. In 2004, the Irish pop "supergroup" U2 asked Apple to help promote their new single "Vertigo." They realized that Apple technology would increase their appeal to younger fans.

U2 were in a commercial for iPod, but

they did not get an appearance fee. They were going to earn money in two other ways. First, the commercial would help their new record sell. Second, Apple had designed a special U2 black and red iPod, and the band members were getting a royalty for every one that was sold.

Shadows of cancer

In 1997, when Jobs was running both Apple and Pixar at the same time, he worked very, very hard. He got so tired that he developed kidney stones. In October 2003, his doctor asked him to get a kidney scan.

The scan showed that his kidneys were fine but that there was a shadow on his pancreas. When the doctors checked his pancreas, they found a cancer tumor. All Jobs's friends advised him to have an operation as soon as possible, but as a true hippie, he wanted to try "alternative" therapies first.

He started a special diet (no meat, fish, eggs or dairy products, and only carrot juice and fruit juice to drink). He also had acupuncture and herbal medicine treatments. Nine months later, in July 2004, Jobs had a second scan. The tumor had got bigger.

Finally, Jobs had an operation. When the doctors cut out part of his pancreas, they found that the cancer had spread to his liver. Jobs told everybody he was okay now, but he had to start having chemotherapy.

Jobs was very strong-willed and always did exactly what he wanted. Some people think that if he had taken other people's advice and had the operation earlier, he might still be alive today.

Jobs's thoughts on death

The year after his operation, Steve made a speech at Stanford University. He talked to the students about what death meant to him.

Steve Jobs speaks at the graduation ceremony at Stanford University, in Palo Alto, California, Sunday, June 12, 2005.

Photo: AP Photo

For the past 33 years, I have looked in the mirror every morning and asked myself: "If today were the last day of my life, would I want to do what I am about to do today?" And whenever the answer has been "No" for too many days in a row, I know I need to change something.

Remembering that I'll be dead soon is the most important tool I've ever encountered to help me make the big choices in life. ... Remembering that you are going to die is the best way I know to avoid the trap of thinking you have something to lose. You are already naked. There is no reason not to follow your heart.

Your time is limited, so don't waste it living someone else's life. Don't be trapped by dogma —which is living with the results of other people's thinking. Don't let the noise of others' opinions drown out your own inner voice. And most important, have the courage to follow your heart and intuition. They somehow already know what you truly want to become.

The success of Pixar

Apple was doing well, and so was Steve's other company, Pixar. After *Toy Story*, it produced *A Bug's Life* in 1998, *Toy Story 2* in 1999, *Monsters, Inc.* in 2001, *Finding Nemo* in 2003, and *The Incredibles* in 2004. All these films earned millions of dollars, with *Finding Nemo* making $870 million worldwide.

Pixar's partner, Disney, was not having much success with its own animated films, so when Bob Iger became Disney CEO in 2005, he decided to buy Pixar. Disney paid $7.4 billion dollars for the company. Because Disney paid with stock, Jobs became Disney's biggest shareholder with 7% of the company.

Jobs was careful to protect Pixar's independence after the takeover. He was worried that if it just became a part of a big corporation, it might lose its magic. Disney had bought Pixar, but Pixar controlled the Disney animation department. Pixar also kept its own offices separate from Disney.

The origins of the iPhone

Jobs noticed that people had stopped using point-and-shoot digital cameras. Why? Because everyone was taking pictures with the cameras in their mobile phones. Jobs realized that the same thing could happen to Apple's iPod. If somebody built a mobile phone with a good music player, iPods could stop selling very fast.

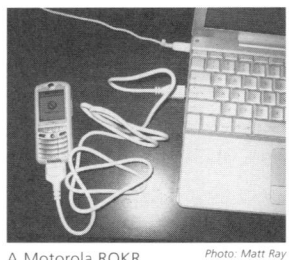

A Motorola ROKR cell phone
Photo: Matt Ray

Most companies don't want to make new products that compete with their existing products. But Jobs knew that if Apple didn't make a music mobile phone, some other company would.

So Apple teamed up with Motorola, a telecommunications company, to make an iTunes phone called the ROKR ("rocker" as in "rock'n'roll"). The reaction when it came out in September 2005 was quite negative. Transferring songs from a computer to the ROKR phone was slow, and the phone could only hold 100 songs.

Do it yourself

Jobs decided that Apple could make a better

mobile phone than any phone company. While working with Motorola, Apple also started developing its own mobile phone.

In the beginning, the Apple team members were not sure how to design their phone. Should they use the same Click Wheel as on the iPod? Or would a touchscreen be better?

After a few months, they decided on touchscreen technology. Jobs bought a company called FingerWorks that had been founded by two scientists from the University of Delaware. They had developed multi-touch technology that responded to the way people moved their fingers on the glass.

A completely new design

Having multi-touch meant that Apple's phone would not need a keyboard. It would have the simplicity Jobs always aimed for. But that wasn't enough. Jobs also wanted a design that felt completely different from that of other mobile phones.

In those days, most cell phones felt cheap, light, and plastic. Jobs wanted to make the Apple phone feel special. He decided that a glass screen would make the phone more elegant, but because people often drop phones, Apple needed glass that would not break easily.

Jobs heard about a company in New York called Corning Glass. Corning had developed a very strong glass called "gorilla glass" in the 1960s. No one had wanted the glass, so the company was not making it.

Jobs ordered tons and tons of gorilla glass from Corning. The boss of Corning was shocked. "We don't have any factories that are making it," he said. "We can't do it."

Jobs looked the boss of Corning in the eye. "Don't be afraid. You can do it," he said. Jobs did not believe that anything was impossible. If you wanted something to happen, you could make it happen. His charisma worked. The boss of Corning agreed, and in less than six months, his company was manufacturing a glass they had never mass-produced before.

The launch of the iPhone

Steve Jobs launched the iPhone at Macworld in January 2007. As usual, he made a great presentation.

> *Every once in a while a revolutionary product comes along that changes everything. Apple has been able to introduce a few of these into the world. In 1984 we introduced the Macintosh. It didn't just change Apple, it changed the whole industry. In 2001 we introduced the first iPod, and it didn't just change the way we all listened to music, it changed the entire music industry.*
>
> *Today we're introducing THREE revolutionary products of this class. The first one is a widescreen iPod with touch controls.*

> *The second is a revolutionary mobile phone. And the third is a breakthrough internet communications device.*
>
> *These are not three separate devices, this is one device, and we are calling it iPhone.*

People said the $500 iPhone was too expensive, just like the iPod. But just like the iPod it was very, very popular.

Three generations: iPhone original, 3G and 3GS (left to right)

A liver transplant

One year later, Steve introduced the iPhone 3G at the Worldwide Developers Conference in June 2008. The audience liked the new phone, but they were shocked at how thin Steve was. Because of the cancer, it was difficult for him to eat. Finally, in January 2009, he had to stop going to work at Apple.

His doctors told him he needed a liver transplant. They put his name on the waiting list for a liver in California, the state where he lived, and also in Tennessee. (To get on the waiting list for a transplant, you need to be able to reach the hospital in eight hours. Because Jobs had a plane, he could get to Tennessee quickly, even though it was 3,400 kilometers from his home.)

Jobs was very weak when the phone rang on March 21, 2009. "There's been a car accident," the doctor told him. "A young man has died, and you can have his liver." The transplant operation was a success. After three months of rest, Jobs went back to Apple at the end of June.

Jobs was sick, but the company was still busy making amazing new products. The next one to come out was the iPad.

The iPad

There are different stories about the origin of the iPad. Some people say that Jobs had the idea for it when he went to dinner with a Microsoft engineer. The man talked for hours and hours about the tablet PC he was making at Microsoft. But the Microsoft tablet used a stylus. Jobs thought people should use their fingers, not a stylus. He was so angry that he decided to make an Apple tablet to show that touch control was better.

Other people say that Jonathan Ive had the idea of a computer with a touchscreen keyboard as the best way to compete with small, light netbooks.

Steve Jobs holds the new iPad in San Francisco, California, January 27, 2010. *Photo: Kyodo News*

The Return of the King

At the January 2010 event where Jobs first showed the iPad, he presented it as a "third category device." The iPad was better than a laptop or a smartphone for things like reading and browsing the Internet.

The first reaction was not that positive. Some journalists said the iPad was just a giant iPhone. But when it went on sale on April 5, it was another big hit. One million iPads sold in the first month.

With the iPod, Steve Jobs had changed the music business. Now with the iPad, he was going to change publishing. Magazines and newspapers that had made the mistake of putting their content up for free on the Internet realized they could charge for the same content on the iPad.

Big Brother Apple

In the 1970s and 1980s, Apple was a small, young, and rebellious company fighting against the giant IBM. In the 1990s, it was a small company fighting against the giant Microsoft. But after the year 2000, Apple was getting bigger and more profitable every year.

Apple started to control the content of applications on the iPad and the iPhone. (Pornography and provocative political content were not allowed.) It also refused to have Adobe Flash (software for playing online video) on the iPhone or iPad.

Then in April 2010, an Apple engineer accidentally left a prototype of the new iPhone 4 in a bar near the company's office. Two men found the phone and sold it to a journalist at Gizmodo, a technology website. The police then raided the house of the journalist. It was big news. Good little Apple had become a bully, a wicked "Big Brother"!

Despite this episode and also some problems with its antenna, the iPhone 4 was another big hit when it came out in June 2010.

Jobs's last act

Toward the end of 2010, Jobs's health was getting worse. He was hardly eating anything. In January 2011, he took medical leave from Apple again.

He started meeting various people for the last time. His visitors included his daughter Lisa, Larry Page of Google, former U.S. president Bill Clinton, and Bill Gates.

In March 2011, even though he was very thin and weak, Jobs did a presentation for the new iPad 2 in San Francisco. In June 2011, he also unveiled iCloud, a remote content storage system.

Weak though he was, he was still dreaming of the future. With the famous British architect Sir Norman Foster, Jobs was planning a new headquarters building for Apple. He was also getting a beautiful boat built in the Netherlands for his family.

By July 2011, the cancer had moved into

Jobs's bones. Knowing he was going to die soon, he wanted to make sure he chose the best person to lead Apple. As a boy, Jobs had admired Hewlett-Packard. He wanted to build a company that would last a long time, too. Handing over power to the best leader was important.

At a board meeting on August 24, Jobs resigned. He chose Tim Cook to be the next CEO.

A great man is gone

Less than two months later, on October 5, 2011, Steve Jobs died at home, surrounded by his family. Apple announced his death with this press release:

We are deeply saddened to announce that Steve Jobs passed away today.

Steve's brilliance, passion and energy were the source of countless innovations that enrich and improve all of our lives. The world is immeasurably better because of Steve.

His greatest love was for his wife, Laurene, and his family. Our hearts go out to them and to all who were touched by his extraordinary gifts.

On the company website, Apple put up a black and white photograph of Jobs with the following words.

Apple has lost a visionary and creative genius, and the world has lost an amazing human being. Those of us who have been fortunate enough to know and work with Steve have lost a dear friend and an inspiring mentor. Steve leaves behind a company that only he could have built, and his spirit will forever be the foundation of Apple.

Word List

- 本文で使われている全ての語を掲載しています（LEVEL 1, 2）。ただし、LEVEL 3 以上は、中学校レベルの語を含みません。
- 語形が規則変化する見出しは原形で示しています。不規則変化語は本文中で使われている形になっています。
- 一般的な意味を紹介していますので、一部の語で本文中で実際に使われている品詞や意味と合っていないことがあります。
- 品詞は以下のように示しています。

名 名詞	代 代名詞	形 形容詞	副 副詞	動 動詞	助 助動詞
前 前置詞	接 接続詞	間 間投詞	冠 冠詞	略 略語	俗 俗語
頭 接頭語	尾 接尾辞	記 記号	関 関係代名詞		

A

- **A player** 一番仕事ができる人材
- **Abdulfattah Jandali** アブドゥルファター・ジャンダリ《実の父親》
- **about to** 《be－》まさに～しようとしている、～するところだ
- **above** 熟 put ～ above … ～を…より優先させる
- **academic** 形 ①学校の、大学の ②学問の
- **Academy Award** アカデミー賞《米国の映画賞》
- **accent** 名 アクセント、口調、特徴
- **accept** 動 ①受け入れる ②同意する、認める
- **accident** 名 ①(不慮の)事故、災難 ②偶然
- **account** 名 勘定、帳簿 do accounts 帳簿をつける
- **achieve** 動 成し遂げる、達成する、成功を収める
- **act** 名 行為、行い 動 ①行動する ②機能する ③演じる
- **actually** 副 実際に、本当に、実は
- **acupuncture** 名 鍼、鍼治療
- **add** 動 加える、足す
- **admire** 動 感心する、賞賛する
- **Adobe Flash** アドビ フラッシュ《Adobe Systems社による、動画やゲームなどを扱うための規格及びそれを制作するソフトウェア群の名称》
- **adopt** 動 養子にする
- **adoption** 名 養子縁組 put up someone for adoption (人)を養子に出す
- **advantage** 名 有利な点[立場]、強み、優越 take advantage of ～を利用する、～につけ込む
- **advertisement** 名 広告、宣伝
- **advertising** 名 広告、宣伝 形 広告の
- **advice** 名 忠告、助言、意見
- **advisor** 名 忠告者、助言者、顧問
- **Africa** 名 アフリカ《大陸》
- **after** 熟 after that その後 look after ～の世話をする、～に気をつける
- **age** 熟 at the age of ～歳のときに
- **agency** 名 代理店、代行会社
- **aggression** 名 攻撃性、好戦的なこと[性質]
- **aggressive** 形 ①攻撃的な、好戦的な ②強引な

WORD LIST

- **Ahwahnee** 名 アワニー《ホテル名》
- **aim** 動 ねらう, 目指す
- **all** 熟 all one's life ずっと, 生まれてから first of all まず第一に
- **allow** 動 ①許す, 《 — ... to 〜》…が〜するのを可能にする, …に〜させておく ②与える
- **along** 熟 get along with (人)と仲良くする《付き合う》
- **alternative** 形 代わりの, 代替の 名 代替え手段, 代替案
- **although** 接 〜だけれども, 〜にもかかわらず, たとえ〜でも
- **amazing** 形 驚くべき, 見事な
- **Amelio, Gil** ギル・アメリオ《企業家, アップルコンピュータ元CEO。在職1994-1997》
- **American** 形 アメリカ(人)の 名 アメリカ人
- **and so** そこで, それだから, それで
- **Andy** 名 アンディ《アニメーション映画『Toy Story』の登場人物》
- **animated** 形 アニメの
- **animation** 名 アニメーション, 動画
- **announce** 動 (人に)知らせる, 公表する
- **annual** 形 年1回の, 例年の, 年次の
- **another** 熟 one another お互い
- **antenna** 名 アンテナ
- **anymore** 副 《通例否定文, 疑問文で》今はもう, これ以上, これから
- **appeal** 名 ①要求, 訴え ②魅力, 人気
- **appearance fee** 出演料
- **Apple** 名 アップル社《社名, 正式名称は Apple Inc.》
- **Apple Computer** アップルコンピュータ社《旧社名, 2007年に Apple Inc.に改称》
- **Apple I** 名 Apple I (アップル ワン)《アップルコンピュータ社が最初に開発したコンピュータ, 1976》
- **Apple II** 名 Apple II (アップル ツー)《世界で初めて個人向けに大量生産・大量販売されたマイクロコンピュータ, 1977》
- **Apple Store** アップルストア《アップル社の直営店》
- **application** 名 アプリケーションソフトウエア
- **approach** 名 やり方
- **architect** 名 建築家, 設計者
- **argument** 名 議論, 論争
- **arrange** 動 ①並べる, 整える ②取り決める ③準備する, 手はずを整える
- **arrogant** 形 尊大な, 傲慢な, 無礼な, 横柄な
- **artwork** 名 アートワーク, 芸術作品
- **as** 熟 as 〜 as possible できるだけ〜 as a result その結果(として) as a whole 全体として as it is 実際は, 〜実際 as soon as 〜するとすぐ, 〜するや否や as usual いつものように, 相変わらず as well as 〜と同様に
- **ask 〜 if** 〜かどうか尋ねる
- **assemble** 動 集める
- **assistant** 名 助手, 補佐
- **associate** 動 〜を連想する
- **Atari** 名 アタリ《社名, アメリカのビデオゲーム会社》
- **attack** 動 ①襲う, 攻める ②非難する
- **attend** 動 出席する
- **attitude** 名 姿勢, 態度
- **attractive** 形 魅力的な, あいきょうのある
- **audience** 名 聴衆, 視聴者
- **automate** 動 自動化する

- **available** 形 利用［使用・入手］できる, 得られる
- **Avenue** 名 〜通り, 〜街
- **avoid** 動 避ける, (〜を)しないようにする
- **award** 名 賞, 賞品

B

- **B player** (一番仕事ができるA Playerに比べて)少し劣る人材
- **b.** 略 born (bear (生まれる)の過去分詞)の略
- **baby** 熟 have a baby 赤ちゃんを産む
- **back** 熟 fight back 反撃に転じる, 応戦する get 〜 back 〜を取り返す[戻す] get back 戻る, 帰る pay back 返済する, お返しをする take back 取り戻す
- **background** 名 背景, 前歴, 生い立ち
- **badly** 副 ①悪く, まずく, へたに ②とても, ひどく
- **balance** 名 均衡
- **band** 名 楽団, バンド
- **bar** 名 酒場
- **barefoot** 形 はだしの, 素足の
- **base** 動《 – on 〜》〜に基礎を置く, 基づく
- **based on** 《be – 》〜に基づく
- **bath** 熟 take a bath 風呂に入る
- **bathe** 動 風呂に入る
- **bay** 名 湾, 入り江
- **Bay Area** ベイエリア《(サンフランシスコ)湾岸地帯》
- **Be Inc.** 名 Be Inc. (ビー社)《コンピュータハードウェア及びソフトウェア製造企業, 1990–2001》
- **bear** 動 ①耐える ②(子を)産む
- **Beatles, the** ザ・ビートルズ《イギリスのロックバンド, 1960–1970》
- **become fascinated with** 〜に心を奪われる
- **been** 熟 have been to 〜へ行ったことがある
- **beginner** 名 初心者
- **beginning** 名 初め, 始まり
- **behave** 動 振る舞う
- **behind** 前 ①〜の後ろに, 〜の背後に ②〜に遅れて, 〜に劣って 副 ①後ろに, 背後に ②遅れて, 劣って leave behind あとにする, 〜を置き去りにする
- **beige** 形 ベージュ色の
- **Berkeley** 名 カリフォルニア大学バークレー校
- **Bertelsmann** 名 ベルテルスマン《ドイツに本社を置くメディア・コングロマリット》
- **best-selling** 形 ベストセラーの
- **better** 熟 even better さらに素晴らしいことに
- **big** 熟 be no bigger than 〜ほどの大きさだ
- **Big Brother** 独裁者
- **Bill Clinton** ビル・クリントン《アメリカ第42代大統領, 在任 1993–2001》
- **Bill Fernandez** ビル・フェルナンデス《ジョブズとウォズニアックの学生時代の共通の友人でアップルコンピュータの従業員第一号》
- **Bill Gates** ビル・ゲイツ《William Henry Gates III, マイクロソフト社の共同創業者・会長, 1955–》
- **Bill Hewlett** ビル・ヒューレット《ヒューレット・パッカードの共同創業者, 1913–2001》
- **billion** 形 10億の, ばく大な, 無数の 名 10億
- **billionaire** 名 億万長者
- **birth** 名 ①出産, 誕生 ②生まれ, 起源, (よい)家柄 give birth to 〜を生

Word List

む
- **bite** 名 かむこと, かみ傷, ひと口
- **Blade Runner** 『ブレード・ランナー』《映画, 1982》
- **blonde** 名 金髪の女性, ブロンドの女性
- **Blue Box** ブルー・ボックス《不正に無料で長距離電話をかける装置》
- **board** 名 取締役会, 重役会
- **Bob Dylan** ボブ・ディラン《アメリカのミュージシャン, 1941–》
- **Bob Iger** ボブ・アイガー《ディズニー社CEO, 1951–》
- **bone** 名 骨, 《-s》骨格
- **bonus** 名 ボーナス, おまけ
- **bookkeeper** 名 簿記係
- **bored** 動 bore (退屈させる) の過去, 過去分詞 形 うんざりした, 退屈した
- **boring** 形 うんざりさせる, 退屈な
- **boss** 名 上司, 親方, 監督
- **Boston** 名 ボストン《地名》
- **bottom** 名 底, 下部
- **box** 熟 out of the box 買ったその日から使える
- **bozo** 名 ばか者, 愚か者
- **brand** 名 ブランド, 商標
- **Braun** 名 ブラウン《ドイツに本拠を置く小型電気器具メーカー》
- **breakthrough** 名 突破, 打開, ブレークスルー
- **breathe** 動 ①呼吸する ②ひと息つく, 休息する
- **breed** 名 品種, 血統
- **brilliance** 名 ①輝き, 光沢 ②優れた才能, 明敏さ
- **bring back** 戻す, 呼び戻す, 持ち帰る
- **British** 形 英国人の 名 英国人
- **browse** 動 (インターネットの情報を) 閲覧する

- **brushed steel** ブラッシュドスチール《ブラッシュド加工 (表面に左右に流れるような研磨あとをつける) したスチール》
- **Buddhism** 名 仏教, 仏道, 仏法
- **Bug's Life** 『バグズ・ライフ』《ディズニー＆ピクサーにより制作されたフルCGアニメーション映画, 1998》
- **building** 動 build (建てる) の現在分詞 名 建物, 建造物, ビルディング
- **bully** 名 いじめっ子
- **business-minded** 形 職業意識のある
- **businessman** 名 ビジネスマン, 実業家
- **but** 熟 not ~ but … ～ではなくて…
- **Buzz Lightyear** バズ・ライトイヤー《アニメーション映画『Toy Story』の登場人物》

C

- **cafeteria** 名 カフェテリア, 社員食堂
- **calculator** 名 計算機, 電卓
- **California** 名 カリフォルニア《米国の州》
- **calligraphy** 名 書道, 習字 (= Japanese calligraphy)
- **calm** 形 穏やかな, 落ち着いた
- **camera** 名 カメラ
- **campaign** 名 キャンペーン (活動, 運動)
- **cancer** 名 癌
- **candle** 名 ろうそく
- **Canon** 名 キヤノン株式会社《日本の電気機器メーカー》
- **capacity** 名 ①定員, 容量 ②能力, (潜在的な) 可能性

- **CAPS** 略 Computer Animation Production System《ディズニー＆ピクサーによるコンピュータとソフトを使ったアニメーション作画システム》の略
- **car crash** 自動車事故
- **care** 熟 **take care** 気をつける, 注意する **take care of** ～の世話をする, ～面倒を見る, ～を管理する
- **carrot** 名 ニンジン（人参）
- **catch up** 追い上げる
- **category** 名 カテゴリー, 種類
- **Catmull, Ed** エド・キャットムル《コンピュータ科学者, ピクサー社長, 1945–》
- **cell phone** 携帯電話
- **cemetery** 名 共同墓地
- **cent** 名 セント《米国などの通貨単位。1ドルの100分の1》
- **CEO** 略 最高経営責任者（= Chief Executive Officer）
- **ceremony** 名 儀式, 式典
- **certainly** 副 確かに, 必ず
- **chairman** 名 委員長, 会長, 議長
- **challenge** 名 挑戦
- **chaotic** 形 大混乱の, 雑然とした, 混沌とした
- **character** 名 ①特性, 個性 ②（小説・劇などの）登場人物 ③品性, 人格
- **charge** 動（代金を）請求する **charge for** ～の料金として請求する 名 責任 **in charge of** ～を任されて, ～を担当して, ～の責任を負って
- **charisma** 名 カリスマ性
- **charm** 名 魅力, 魔力
- **charming** 形 魅力的な, チャーミングな
- **check** 動 検査する
- **chemotherapy** 名 化学療法
- **chief** 名 頭, 長
- **chip** 名 チップ, 半導体素子, 集積回路
- **choice** 名 選択（の範囲・自由）, 選ばれた人［物］ **lifestyle choice** 生活様式の選択肢
- **Chrisann Brennan** クリスアン・ブレナン《最初のガールフレンド》
- **Christian** 名 キリスト教徒, クリスチャン
- **Christmas** 名 クリスマス
- **Clara Jobs** クララ・ジョブズ《養母, 1924–1986》
- **clear** 形 はっきりした, 明白な
- **clerk** 名 事務員, 店員
- **click** 名（マウスの）クリック
- **Click Wheel** クリックホイール《iPodシリーズに搭載されている操作インタフェース。ドーナツ状のタッチパッドの中心に円形のボタンが配置され片手で様々な操作が可能》
- **clothing** 名 衣類, 衣料品
- **co-produce** 動 ～を共同制作する
- **coast** 名 海岸, 沿岸
- **collapse** 名 崩壊, 倒壊
- **colleague** 名 同僚
- **colorful** 形 カラフルな, 派手な
- **combination** 名 ①結合（状態, 行為）, 団結 ②連合, 同盟
- **come along** ①一緒に来る, ついて来る ②やって来る, 現れる ③うまくいく, よくなる, できあがる
- **come out** 出てくる, 出掛ける, 姿を現す, 発行される
- **come up** 近づいてくる, 階上に行く, 浮上する, 水面へ上ってくる, 発生する, 芽を出す
- **comment** 動 論評する, 注解する, コメントする
- **commercial** 名 コマーシャル
- **common sense** 常識, 共通感覚
- **commune** 名 コミューン, 生活共同体

WORD LIST

- **communication** 名 伝えること, 伝導, 連絡
- **Compaq** 名 コンパック《パーソナルコンピュータ企業, 2002年にヒューレット・パッカード社に吸収合併される。1892–2002》
- **compete** 動 ①競争する ②匹敵する
- **competition** 名 競争, 競合, コンペ
- **competitor** 名 競争相手, 競争者
- **complain** 動 ①不平［苦情］を言う, ぶつぶつ言う ②（病状などを）訴える
- **complete** 形 完全な, まったくの, 完成した
- **completely** 副 完全に, すっかり
- **component** 名 構成要素, 部品, 成分
- **Computer Animation Production System** （ディズニー＆ピクサーによる）コンピュータとソフトを使ったアニメーション作画システム
- **computer-generated** 形 コンピュータで作った, CGの
- **computing** 名 コンピュータの使用
- **concentrate** 動 一点に集める［集まる］, 集中させる［する］
- **concept** 名 ①概念, 観念, テーマ ②（計画案などの）基本的な方向
- **concierge service** 接客サービス
- **conduct** 動 ①指導する ②実施する
- **conference** 名 ①会議, 協議, 相談 ②協議会
- **confidence** 名 自信, 確信, 信頼, 信用度
- **connect** 動 つながる, つなぐ, 関係づける
- **connection** 名 ①つながり, 関係 ②縁故
- **consider** 動 考慮する, 〜しようと思う
- **consumer** 名 消費者
- **content** 名 ①《-s》中身, 内容
- **contest** 名 （〜を目指す）競争
- **contrast** 名 対照, 対比
- **control** 動 ①管理［支配］する ②抑制する, コントロールする 名 ①管理, 支配（力） ②抑制
- **Cook, Tim** ティム・クック《アップル社CEO》
- **copy** 動 写す, まねる, コピーする
- **Corning (Glass)** コーニング《アメリカのガラス製品メーカー》
- **corporate** 形 団体［共同］の, 会社の
- **corporation** 名 法人, (株式)会社
- **cost** 動 (金・費用が)かかる, (〜を)要する, (人に金額を)費やさせる
- **could have done** 〜だったかもしれない《仮定法》
- **counter** 名 カウンター, 計算器
- **countless** 形 無数の, 数え切れない
- **county** 名 郡, 州
- **couple** 名 ①2つ, 対 ②夫婦, 一組
- **courage** 名 勇気, 度胸
- **cowboy** 名 カウボーイ, 牧童, 牛飼い
- **craftsman** 名 職人, 熟練工
- **craftsmanship** 名 職人の技
- **crash** 名 激突 car crash 自動車事故
- **crazy** 形 ①狂気の, ばかげた, 無茶な ②夢中の, 熱狂的な
- **create** 動 創造する, 生み出す, 引き起こす
- **creative** 形 創造力のある, 独創的な
- **creator** 名 創作者, 創造者, 神

- **criticism** 名 批評, 非難, 反論, 評論
- **crowd** 名 群集, 雑踏, 多数, 聴衆
- **cube** 名 立方体
- **cupboard** 名 食器棚, 戸棚
- **current** 形 現在の, 目下の
- **customer** 名 顧客
- **cut out** 切り取る, 切り抜く

D

- **dairy product** 乳製品, 酪農製品
- **day** 熟 in those days あのころは, 当時は one day (過去の)ある日, (未来の)いつか
- **de** 冠 the のドイツ語訛り風発音
- **deal** 名 ①取引, 扱い ②(不特定の)量, 額 a good [great] deal (of ~) かなり[ずいぶん・大量](の~), 多額(の~) make a deal with ~と取引する term of deal 契約条件
- **death** 名 死, 死ぬこと
- **deeply** 副 深く, 非常に
- **delicate** 形 繊細な, 壊れやすい
- **department** 名 部門
- **deposit** 名 預かり金, 保証金
- **description** 名 (言葉で)記述(すること), 描写(すること)
- **design** 動 設計する, 企てる 名 デザイン, 設計(図)
- **designed** 形 設計された
- **designer** 名 デザイナー, 設計者
- **desk lamp** 電気スタンド
- **desktop** 名 机の上, 卓上
- **desktop (personal) computer** デスクトップ・コンピュータ, デスクトップパソコン
- **despite** 前 ~にもかかわらず
- **detective** 名 探偵
- **develop** 動 ①発達する[させる] ②開発する
- **developer** 名 開発者, 宅地開発業者, デベロッパー
- **device** 名 ①工夫 ②案 ③装置
- **diagram** 名 図表, 図式, 図解
- **Diana, Princess** ダイアナ元英皇太子妃《1961–1997》
- **diet** 名 ①食べ物, 食事 ②食習慣 ③ダイエット, 食餌療法
- **Dieter Rams** ディーター・ラムス《ドイツのインダストリアルデザイナー, 1932–》
- **differently** 副 (~と)異なって, 違って
- **digital** 形 ①数字の, 数字表示の, デジタルの ②指の, 指状の
- **digital hub** デジタルハブ《デジタル製品の中心にあって, それらを接続したり, データを交換したりする機器》
- **director** 名 管理者, 指導者, 監督
- **disagreeable** 形 不愉快な, 付き合いにくい
- **disaster** 名 災害, 災難, まったくの失敗
- **disk** 名 円盤(状の物) hard disk ハードディスク・ドライブ, 固定磁気ディスク装置
- **Disney** 名 ディズニー社《社名, 正式名称 The Walt Disney Company》
- **display** 名 表示 text display 文字表示
- **divide** 動 分かれる, 分ける, 割れる, 割る divide into ~に分かれる be divided into 分けられる
- **division** 名 部門
- **divorce** 動 離婚する get divorced 離婚する
- **DNA** 略 デオキシリボ核酸《生物の遺伝情報を担う物質》
- **do well** 成績が良い, 成功する
- **document** 名 文書, 記録
- **dogma** 名 ①教義, ドグマ ②独断

Word List

的な考え
- **download** 動 ~をダウンロードする《ホストコンピュータに記録されているデータやプログラムを別のコンピュータに取り込むこと》
- **dramatic** 形 劇的な、印象的な、劇の
- **dramatically** 副 劇的に、芝居がかったしぐさで
- **drew** 動 draw（引く）の過去
- **drop out of** ~を途中でやめる
- **drown out** （大きな音が小さな音を）かき消す
- **drug** 名 薬、麻薬
- **dying** 形 死にかかっている

E

- **e-mail** 名 電子メール
- **eager** 形 ①熱心な ②《be – for ~》~を切望している、《be – to ~》しきりに~したがっている
- **earn** 動 ①儲ける、稼ぐ ②（名声を）博す
- **easily** 副 ①容易に、たやすく、苦もなく ②気楽に
- **East Coast** イースト・コースト、東海岸
- **easy-to-understand** 形 理解しやすい、分かりやすい
- **Ed Catmull** エド・キャットマル《コンピュータ科学者、ピクサー社長、1945–》
- **edge** 名 端、縁
- **edit** 動 編集する
- **education** 名 教育、教養
- **educational** 形 教育（上）の
- **effect** 名 影響、効果 **film effect** フィルム効果
- **effective** 形 効果的である、有効である
- **efficient** 形 ①効率的な、有効な ②有能な、敏腕な
- **Eichler, Joseph** ジョセフ・アイクラー《不動産開発業者、1900–1970》
- **either A or B** AかそれともB
- **electronic** 形 電子工学の、エレクトロニクスの
- **electronics** 名 エレクトロニクス、電子工学、電子機器
- **elegant** 形 上品な、優雅な
- **elementary** 形 ①初歩の ②単純な、簡単な
- **else** 熟 **no one else** 他の誰一人として~しない
- **EMI** 名 EMI《イギリスのレコード会社》
- **empathy** 名 共感、感情移入
- **encounter** 動 （思いがけなく）出会う、遭う
- **end** 熟 **at the end of** ~の終わりに **in the end** とうとう、結局、ついに
- **enemy** 名 敵
- **engineer** 名 技師
- **engineering** 名 工学
- **English-style** 形 英国式の
- **enlightenment** 名 啓発、啓蒙、教化
- **enrich** 動 豊かにする、充実させる
- **enroll** 動 登録する、入会する、入学する
- **entertainment** 名 楽しみ、娯楽、エンターテイメント
- **entire** 形 全体の、完全な、まったくの
- **entrepreneur** 名 企業家、起業家
- **episode** 名 挿話、出来事
- **equipment** 名 装置、機材、道具、設備
- **Erin** 名 エリン《ジョブズの娘》
- **Esslinger, Hartmut** ハートムート・エスリンガー《インダストリア

ルデザイナー, 1944–》
- **Europe** 名 ヨーロッパ
- **Eve** 名 イブ《ジョブズの娘》
- **even better** さらに素晴らしいことに
- **even if** たとえ〜でも
- **even though** 〜であるけれども, 〜にもかかわらず
- **event** 熟 turn of events 出来事の節目
- **everybody** 代 誰でも, 皆
- **everyday** 形 毎日の, 日々の
- **everyone** 代 誰でも, 皆
- **everything** 代 すべてのこと[もの], 何でも, 何もかも
- **everywhere** 副 どこにいても, いたるところに
- **Excel** 名（マイクロソフト・)エクセル《Microsoft Excel, 表計算ソフト。GUIでの利用を前提にMacintosh用アプリケーションソフトウェアとして開発された》
- **except** 前 〜を除いて, 〜のほかは
- **excited** 形 興奮した, わくわくした
- **executive** 名 重役, 役員, 幹部
- **exist** 動 存在する, 生存する, ある, いる
- **experiment** 動 実験する, 試みる
- **expert** 名 専門家, 熟練者, エキスパート
- **Explorers Club, Hewlett-Packard** ヒューレット・パッカード・エクスプローラーズ・クラブ《HP社のエンジニア有志が火曜日の夜に社内のカフェテリアで開いていた情報交換会》
- **extraordinary** 形 異常な, 並はずれた, 驚くべき
- **extreme** 形 極端な, 極度の, いちばん端の
- **eye** 熟 look someone in the eye （人）の目を直視する

F

- **Facebook** 名 フェイスブック《Facebook, Inc.の提供する, SNS（ソーシャル・ネットワーキング・サービス)》
- **fact** 熟 in fact つまり, 実は, 要するに
- **factory** 名 工場, 製造所
- **fail** 動 失敗する, 落second する[させる]
- **Fairchild** 名 フェアチャイルド（セミコンダクター)《Fairchild semiconductor, アメリカの半導体メーカー》
- **fall in love with** 恋におちる
- **far too** あまりにも〜過ぎる
- **fascinated** 形 魅了された become fascinated with 〜に心を奪われる
- **fast-growing** 形 急成長している
- **feature** 名 特徴, 特色 動 ①（〜の)特徴になる ②呼び物にする
- **fee** 名 謝礼, 料金
- **feeling** 名 ①感じ, 気持ち ②触感, 知覚 ③同情, 思いやり, 感受性
- **fence** 名 囲み, さく
- **Fernandez, Bill** ビル・フェルナンデス《ジョブズとウォズニアックの学生時代の共通の友人でアップルコンピュータの従業員第一号》
- **Fifth Avenue** 5番街《ニューヨーク市マンハッタンを南北に縦断する「アヴェニュー」と呼ばれる通り。高級マンションや大邸宅が立ち並ぶニューヨークの裕福さの象徴》
- **fight back** 反撃に転じる, 応戦する
- **film** 名 フィルム, 映画 film effect フィルム効果
- **finance** 動 資金を融通する
- **find out** 見つけ出す, 気がつく, 知る, 調べる, 解明する
- **Finding Nemo** 『ファインディ

ング・ニモ』《アニメーション映画, 2003》
- **FingerWorks** 名 フィンガーワークス社《一度に複数のタッチに反応するようデザインされたトラックパッドを開発していた》
- **fire** 動 (人) を解雇する
- **firm** 名 会社
- **first** 熟 at first 最初は, 初めのうちは first of all まず第一に for the first time 初めて
- **first-ever** 形 史上初の, 初めての
- **five-star hotel** 一流ホテル
- **Flash, Adobe** アドビ フラッシュ《Adobe Systems社による, 動画やゲームなどを扱うための規格及び それを制作するソフトウェア群の名称》
- **flashy** 形 ①閃光のような ②派手な, けばけばしい
- **fly to** ～まで飛行機で行く
- **focus** 名 ①焦点, ピント ②関心の的, 着眼点 ③中心 動 ①焦点を合わせる ②(関心・注意を)集中させる
- **folder** 名 フォルダ (紙挟み, 書類ばさみ)
- **following** 形 《the ～》次の, 次に続く
- **font** 名 フォント, 書体
- **force** 名 力, 勢い
- **formal** 形 正式の, 公式の, 形式的な, 格式ばった
- **former** 形 ①前の, 先の, 以前の ②《the ～》(二者のうち)前者の
- **fortunate** 形 幸運な, 幸運をもたらす
- **Fortune 500** フォーチュン500社, 売上規模全米上位500社
- **Foster, Sir Norman** ノーマン・フォスター卿《イギリスの建築家, 1935–》
- **foundation** 名 ①建設, 創設 ②基礎, 土台
- **founder** 名 創立者, 設立者
- **free** 熟 for free 無料で
- **free call** 無料通話
- **frequency** 名 ①頻繁に起こること, 頻発 ②頻度 ③周波数
- **frequency counter** 周波数カウンター
- **Friedland, Robert** ロバート・フリードランド《Ivanhoe Mines (アイバンホー・マインズ, カナダに本社を置く資源企業) 会長。リード大学在籍時, 彼からジョブズは「人を惹き付ける方法」を学んだ》
- **friendly** 形 親しみのある, 親切な, 友情のこもった
- **full-time** 形 常勤の, 専任の
- **fun** 熟 have fun 楽しむ
- **funnily enough** 妙な話だが
- **furnished** 形 家具付きの

G

- **G** 略 ギガバイト《gigabyte = 1,024 メガバイト》の略
- **Gandhi** 名 (マハトマ・) ガンディー《インドの政治指導者, 1869–1948》
- **Gap clothing chain** ギャップ《アメリカ最大の衣料品小売店》
- **garage** 名 (車の)車庫, 修理工場
- **Gates, Bill** ビル・ゲイツ《William Henry Gates III. マイクロソフト社の共同創業者・会長, 1955–》
- **gather** 動 集まる
- **generate** 動 生み出す, 引き起こす
- **genius** 名 天才, 才能
- **Genius Bar** ジーニアスバー《アップルストア内のサービスで, 専門スタッフが製品の技術的な質問に答え, 問題を解決し, 修理を行う》
- **George Lucus** ジョージ・ルーカス《アメリカの映画監督, 映画プロデ

ユーザー, 1944-》
- **George Orwell** ジョージ・オーウェル《イギリスの作家, 1903-1950》
- **German** 形 ドイツ(人・語)の 名 ①ドイツ人 ②ドイツ語
- **Germany** 名 ドイツ《国名》
- **get** 熟 get ～ back ～を取り返す[戻す] get along with (人)と仲良くする[付き合う] get back 戻る, 帰る get divorced 離婚する get on ～に載る, 気が合う get on well うまくやっていく, 肌が合う get someone to do (人)に～させる[してもらう] get started 始める get worse 悪化する
- **giant** 形 巨大な, 偉大な
- **gift** 名 ①贈り物 ②(天賦の)才能
- **gigabyte** 名 ギガバイト《= 1,024メガバイト》
- **Gil Amelio** ギル・アメリオ《企業家, アップルコンピュータ元CEO。在職1994-1997》
- **girlfriend** 名 女友だち
- **give birth to** ～を生む
- **give up** あきらめる, やめる, 引き渡す
- **Gizmodo** ギズモード《インターネットや電化製品などメディアに関連するニュース・話題を扱ったブログメディア》
- **global** 形 地球(上)の, 地球規模の, 世界的な, 国際的な
- **go on sale** 発売される, 市場に出回る
- **go on to** ～に移る, ～に取り掛かる
- **go out** 外出する, 外へ出る
- **go up to** ～まで行く, 近づく
- **God** 名 神《キリスト教》
- **good at** 《be –》～が得意だ
- **good-natured** 形 気だてのよい, 気さくな

- **Google** 名 グーグル《アメリカ合衆国のソフトウェア会社, あるいは, 同社の運営するインターネット上での検索エンジン》
- **gorilla glass** ゴリラガラス《Corningが開発した強化ガラスの名称》
- **got** 熟 have got 持っている have got to ～しなければならない
- **gotten** 動 get (得る)の過去分詞
- **grade** 名 学年
- **gradually** 副 だんだんと
- **graduate** 名 卒業生, (～学校の)出身者
- **graduate student** 大学院生
- **graduating student** 卒業予定者
- **graphic** 形 グラフィックの, 写実的な
- **graphical** 形 グラフィック(図表)による
- **Graphical User Interface** グラフィカルユーザインタフェース《GUI。コンピュータグラフィックスとポインティングデバイスを用いて, 直感的な操作を提供するユーザーインタフェース》
- **graphics** 名 画像, グラフィックス
- **Great Britain** 大ブリテン島《英国の主島》
- **GUI** 略 グラフィカルユーザーインタフェース《Graphical User Interface。コンピュータグラフィックスとポインティングデバイスを用いて, 直感的な操作を提供するユーザーインタフェース》
- **gumdrop** 名 ガムドロップ《菓子》
- **guy** 名 男, やつ《you -s で呼びかけにも用いる》
- **gym** 名 体育館, ジム, スポーツクラブ

WORD LIST

H

- **hacker** 名 ハッカー《①他のコンピュータに不正に侵入する人. ②コンピュータ・マニア》
- **half-complete** 形 半分完成した
- **hall** 名 公会堂, ホール
- **hammer** 名 ハンマー, 金づち
- **hand over** 手渡す, 引き渡す, 譲渡する
- **handheld** 形 手で持って操作できる, ハンドヘルドの
- **handsome** 形 端正な(顔立ちの), りっぱな, (男性が)ハンサムな
- **hard disk** ハードディスク・ドライブ, 固定磁気ディスク装置
- **hard to** ～し難い
- **hardly** 副 ①ほとんど～でない, わずかに ②厳しく, かろうじて
- **hardware** 名 (コンピュータの)ハードウェア
- **Hare Krishna** クリシュナ意識国際協会《新宗教団体》
- **Hartmut Esslinger** ハートムート・エスリンガー《インダストリアルデザイナー, 1944–》
- **have** 熟 could have done ～だったかもしれない《仮定法》have a baby 赤ちゃんを産む have been to ～へ行ったことがある have fun 楽しむ have got ～を持っている have got to ～しなければならない would have … if ～ もし～だったとしたら…しただろう《仮定法》
- **Hawaii** 名 ハワイ《米国の州》
- **headphone** 名 ヘッドフォン
- **headquarters** 名 本社, 本部
- **healthy** 形 健康な, 健全な, 健康によい
- **heaviness** 名 重いこと, 重さ
- **Henry Kissinger** ヘンリー・キッシンジャー《アメリカのニクソン政権およびフォード政権期の国家安全保障問題担当大統領補佐官, 国務長官。1923–》
- **herbal** 形 薬草の, ハーブの, 草の
- **herbal medicine** 植物薬
- **Hewlett-Packard** 名 ヒューレット・パッカード《コンピュータやプリンターなどコンピュータ関連製品の開発・製造・販売行うアメリカの企業。略称HP》
- **Hewlett-Packard Explorers Club** ヒューレット・パッカード・エクスプローラーズ・クラブ《HP社のエンジニア有志が火曜日の夜に社内のカフェテリアで開いていた情報交換会》
- **high school** 高等学校
- **high-tech** 形 ハイテクの, 高度技術の
- **hike** 名 ハイキング
- **hippie** 名 ヒッピー
- **hire** 動 雇う
- **hobby** 名 趣味, 得意なこと
- **hobbyist** 名 愛好家
- **Hollywood** 名 ハリウッド《地名》
- **Homebrew Computer Club** ホームブリュー・コンピュータ・クラブ《「自家醸造」コンピュータ・クラブ》
- **hotspot** 名 ホットスポット《局地的に(何らかの活動が)活発であったりする地点・場所・地域》
- **how to** ～する方法
- **however** 副 たとえ～でも 接 けれども, だが
- **HP** 略 ヒューレット・パッカード(Hewlett-Packard)社の略
- **hub** 名 ハブ, 中央[集線]装置
- **huge** 形 巨大な, ばく大な
- **human being** 人, 人間
- **hunger** 名 空腹, 飢え

THE STEVE JOBS STORY

I

- **IBM** 名 アイビーエム《正式社名 International Business Machines Corporation。コンピュータ関連のサービスおよび製品を提供する企業》
- **iCloud** 名 iCloud（アイクラウド）《アップル社が提供しているクラウドサービス》
- **idiot** 名 ばか、まぬけ
- **if** 熟 ask ～ if ～かどうか尋ねる even if たとえ～でも would have … if ～ もし～だったとしたら…しただろう《仮定法》
- **iMac** 名 iMac（アイマック）《アップル社のパーソナルコンピュータ「Macintosh」のディスプレイ一体型デスクトップ機のシリーズに付けられた名称》
- **image** 名 ①印象、姿 ②画像、映像
- **imagine** 動 想像する、心に思い描く
- **immeasurably** 副 計り知れないほどの、非常に
- **immediately** 副 すぐに、～するやいなや
- **Imogene Hill** イモジェン・ヒル《人名、ジョブズが4年生の時の教師》
- **iMovie** 名 iMovie（アイムービー）《アップル社の「iLife」に含まれるビデオ編集ソフト》
- **importance** 名 重要性、大切さ
- **importantly** 副 重大に、もったいぶって
- **impressed** 副 印象付けられて、感銘を受けて
- **impressive** 形 印象的な、深い感銘を与える
- **improve** 動 改善する［させる］、進歩する
- **impute** 動（収入・利益などの）価値を帰属させる
- **inc.** 略 法人組織の、有限責任の《= incorporated》
- **include** 動 含む、勘定に入れる
- **increase** 動 増加［増強］する、増やす、増える
- **Incredibles, the** 『ミスター・インクレディブル』《ディズニー配給、ピクサー製作のフルCGによるアニメーション映画、2004》
- **indeed** 副 ①実際、本当に ②《強意》まったく
- **independence** 名 独立心、自立
- **India** 名 インド《国名》
- **industrial** 形 工業の、産業の
- **industrial designer** インダストリアル［工業］デザイナー
- **industry** 名 産業、工業
- **influence** 動 影響をおよぼす
- **inner** 形 ①内部の ②心の中の
- **innovation** 名 ①革新、刷新 ②新考案
- **insist** 動 ①主張する、断言する ②要求する
- **inspire** 動 ①奮い立たせる、鼓舞する ②（感情などを）吹き込む ③霊感を与える
- **inspiring** 形 鼓舞する、感激させる
- **integrate** 動 ①統合する、一体化する ②溶け込ませる、溶け込む、差別をなくす
- **Intel** 名 インテル《アメリカの半導体メーカー》
- **intercom** 名 インターコム、インターホン
- **interested** 形 興味を持った、関心のある
- **interface** 名 インターフェース
- **interim** 形 暫定的な、臨時の
- **intuition** 名 直感、洞察
- **invent** 動 発明［考案］する
- **invest** 動 投資する、（金・精力などを）注ぐ
- **investment bank** 投資銀行

Word List

- **investor** 名 出資者, 投資家
- **iPad** 名 iPad（アイパッド）《アップル社製のタブレット型コンピュータ》
- **iPhone** 名 iPhone（アイフォーン）《アップル社製のスマートフォン》
- **iPhoto** 名 iPhoto（アイフォト）《アップル社の「iLife」に含まれる写真管理ソフトウェア》
- **IPO** 略 株式公開《Initial Public Offeringの略. 未上場会社の株式を証券市場において売買可能にすること》
- **iPod** 名 iPod（アイポッド）《アップル社製の携帯型デジタル音楽プレイヤー》
- **Irish** 形 アイルランド(人)の 名 ①アイルランド人 ②アイルランド語
- **It is ~ for someone to ...** （人）が…するのは~だ
- **Italy** 名 イタリア《国名》
- **iTunes** 名 iTunes（アイチューンズ）《アップル社が開発及び配布している動画および音楽の再生・管理ソフト》
- **iTunes store** iTunes Store（アイチューンズ・ストア）《アップル社が運営しているコンテンツ配信サービス》
- **Ive, Jonathan** ジョナサン・アイブ《イギリス人デザイナー, アップル社のインダストリアルデザイングループ担当上級副社長, 1967-》

J

- **Jandali, Abdulfattah** アブドゥルファター・ジャンダーリ《実の父親》
- **Japan** 名 日本《国名》
- **Japanese** 形 日本(人・語)の 名 ①日本人 ②日本語
- **jeans** 名 ジーンズ, ジーパン
- **Jef Raskin** ジェフ・ラスキン《コンピュータ技術者, アップルコンピュータのマッキントッシュの開発を立ち上げた. 1943-2005》
- **Jeffrey Katzenberg** ジェフリー・カッツェンバーグ《アメリカの映画プロデューサー, ドリームワークス・アニメーションSKG最高経営責任者. 1950-》
- **Joanne Scheible** ジョアン・シーブル《実の母親》
- **job title** 仕事の肩書, 職位
- **Jobs** 名 ジョブズ《姓》
- **Jobs, Steve** スティーブ・ジョブズ《アップル社の共同設立者の一人, 1955-2011》
- **jogger** 名 ジョギングする人
- **John Lasseter** ジョン・ラセタ《アメリカの映画監督, アニメーション作家. ウォルト・ディズニー・アニメーション・スタジオ, ピクサー・アニメーション・スタジオ両スタジオのチーフ・クリエイティブ・オフィサー, 1957-》
- **John Lennon** ジョン・レノン《イギリスのミュージシャン. ロックバンド・ビートルズのメンバー, 1940-1980》
- **John McCollum** ジョン・マッカラム《ホームステッドハイスクールでジョブズとスティーブ・ウォズニアックにエレクトロニクスを教えた》
- **John Sculley** ジョン・スカリー《アメリカ実業家. ペプシコーラ社長とアップルコンピュータの社長, CEOを歴任. 1939-》
- **Johnson, Ron** ロン・ジョンソン《ジョブズにターゲット（Target）から引き抜かれ, Apple Storeを約11年間余りでゼロから現在の規模（店舗数300以上, 部門従業員数約3万人）までに育て上げた》
- **Jonathan Ive** ジョナサン・アイブ《イギリス人デザイナー, アップル社のインダストリアルデザイングループ担当上級副社長, 1967-》
- **Joseph Eichler** ジョセフ・アイクラー《不動産開発業者. 1900-1970》

- [ ] **journalist** 名 報道関係者, ジャーナリスト
- [ ] **judge** 動 判決を下す, 裁く, 判断する, 評価する

K

- [ ] **Katzenberg, Jeffrey** ジェフリー・カッツェンバーグ《アメリカの映画プロデューサー。ドリームワークス・アニメーションSKG最高経営責任者。1950–》
- [ ] **key job** 要点職務
- [ ] **keyboard** 名 キーボード
- [ ] **kidney** 名 腎臓
- [ ] **kidney stone** 腎臓結石
- [ ] **kilometer** 名 キロメートル《長さの単位》
- [ ] **knowledge** 名 知識, 理解, 学問

L

- [ ] **lamp** 名 ランプ
- [ ] **laptop** 名 ラップトップコンピュータ, ノート型パソコン
- [ ] **Larry Page** ラリー・ペイジ《Googleの創業者。1973–》
- [ ] **Lasseter, John** ジョン・ラセター《アメリカの映画監督, アニメーション作家。ウォルト・ディズニー・アニメーション・スタジオ, ピクサー・アニメーション・スタジオ両スタジオのチーフ・クリエイティブ・オフィサー。1957–》
- [ ] **latest** 形 最新の, 最近の
- [ ] **launch** 動 (新商品を)売り出す, 発売する 名 (新商品の)売り出し
- [ ] **Laurene Powell** ローレン・パウエル《妻》
- [ ] **lawyer** 名 弁護士, 法律家
- [ ] **layout** 名 配置, レイアウト

- [ ] **leave behind** あとにする, ~を置き去りにする
- [ ] **less** 形 ~より小さい[少ない] 副 ~より少なく, ~ほどでなく
- [ ] **liberal arts** (大学の)一般教養教育[課程]
- [ ] **license** 動 許可を与える
- [ ] **life** 熟 all one's life ずっと, 生まれてから
- [ ] **lifelong** 形 終生の, 生涯続く
- [ ] **lifestyle** 名 生活様式, ライフスタイル lifestyle choice 生活様式の選択肢
- [ ] **lightness** 名 軽いこと, 軽さ
- [ ] **lightweight** 名 軽量級の
- [ ] **like** look like ~のように見える, ~に似ている rather like ~に似ている
- [ ] **limited** 形 限られた, 限定の
- [ ] **Lisa** 名 ①Lisa (リサ)《Apple IIの後継機。1983》②リサ《ジョブズの娘》
- [ ] **list** 名 名簿, 目録, 一覧表 動 (証券を)上場する
- [ ] **Little Mermaid, the** 『リトル・マーメイド』《アニメーション映画。1989》
- [ ] **liver** 名 肝臓
- [ ] **loan** 名 貸付(金), ローン
- [ ] **lobby** 名 ロビー, (玄関)広間
- [ ] **location** 名 位置, 場所
- [ ] **Lockheed** 名 ロッキード《アメリカの航空機メーカー》
- [ ] **logo** 名 ロゴ, 文字, 意匠文字
- [ ] **London** 名 ロンドン《英国の首都》
- [ ] **long-distance** 形 長距離の, 遠く離れた
- [ ] **look after** ~の世話をする, ~に気をつける
- [ ] **look for** ~を探す
- [ ] **look in** 中を見る
- [ ] **look like** ~のように見える, ~に

WORD LIST

似ている
- **look someone in the eye** 〈人〉の目を直視する
- **Los Angeles** ロサンゼルス《米国の都市》
- **lot** 名 敷地, 撮影所, スタジオ
- **love** 熟 fall in love with 恋におちる
- **lover** 名 ①愛人, 恋人 ②愛好者
- **LSD** 名 リセルグ酸ジエチルアミド《幻覚剤》
- **Lucas, George** ジョージ・ルーカス《アメリカの映画監督, 映画プロデューサー, 1944-》
- **Lucasfilm** 名 ルーカスフィルム《1971年にジョージ・ルーカスが設立した映像製作会社》
- **luckily** 副 運よく, 幸いにも

M

- **Mac** 名 Mac（マック）《アップル社が開発および販売するパーソナルコンピュータ, Macintosh（マッキントッシュ）の略称》
- **Macintosh** 名 Macintosh（マッキントッシュ）《アップル社が開発および販売するパーソナルコンピュータ。略称 Mac（マック）》
- **Macworld** 名 マックワールド《米国IDGワールド・エキスポが主催するアップル社の製品に関連した製品の発表や展示が行なわれるイベント》
- **magic** 名 ①魔法, 手品 ②魔力
- **major** 形 大規模な
- **make a deal with** ～と取引する
- **make a mistake** 間違いをする
- **make a speech** 演説をする
- **make into** ～を…に仕立てる
- **make sure** 確かめる, 確認する
- **maker** 名 メーカー
- **manage** 動 ①動かす, うまく処理する ②どうにか～する
- **management** 名 ①経営, 取り扱い ②運営, 管理（側）
- **manager** 名 経営者, 支配人, 支店長, 部長
- **manners** 名 行儀, 作法
- **manufacture** 動 製造［製作］する
- **manufacturing** 名 製造
- **marijuana** 名 マリファナ
- **marketing** 名 マーケティング《製品やサービスの市場調査・開発から販売に至るまでの一連のプロセス》
- **Markkula, Mike** マイク・マークラ《アメリカの企業家。ジョブズとスティーブ・ウォズニアックとともに, Apple Computer社を創立, 1942-》
- **married** 動 marry（結婚する）の過去, 過去分詞 形 結婚した, 既婚の
- **marry** 動 結婚する
- **mass-produced** 形 大量生産された, 大量生産型の
- **matter** 熟 not matter 問題にならない
- **maximum** 名 最大（限）, 最高
- **McKenna, Regis** レジス・マッケンナ《インテル, アップルなどのハイテク企業をクライアントに持つマーケティングコンサルタント》
- **McLean** 名 マクレーン《地名, バージニア州》
- **mechanic** 名 機械工, 修理工
- **media** 名 メディア, マスコミ, 媒体
- **medical** 形 医学の
- **meditation** 名 瞑想, 黙想
- **meeting** 名 集まり, ミーティング
- **memorial service** 告別式, 追悼式
- **memory** 名 ①記憶（力）, 思い出 ②（コンピュータの）メモリ, 記憶装置

- ☐ **mentor** 名 師, 指導者
- ☐ **Mercedes** 名 メルセデス《ドイツのダイムラー社製の高級乗用車》
- ☐ **mermaid** 名 (女の)人魚
- ☐ **Michael Eisner** マイケル・アイズナー《アメリカの実業家。ウォルト・ディズニー・カンパニーCEO, 在職 1984–2005》
- ☐ **Michael Jackson** マイケル・ジャクソン《アメリカのポップシンガー, 1958–2009》
- ☐ **microprocessor** 名 マイクロプロセッサ, 超小型演算装置
- ☐ **Microsoft** 名 マイクロソフト《アメリカに本社を置く世界最大のコンピュータ・ソフトウェア会社》
- ☐ **mid-twenties** 名 20代半ば
- ☐ **middle** 中間, 最中 in the middle of 〜の真ん中[中ほど]に
- ☐ **might** 助 《mayの過去》〜かもしれない
- ☐ **Mike Markkula** マイク・マークラ《アメリカの企業家。ジョブズとスティーブ・ウォズニアックとともに, Apple Computer社を創立, 1942–》
- ☐ **military** 名 《the –》軍, 軍部
- ☐ **Millard Drexler** ミラード・ドレクスラー《米ギャップCEO, 在職 1995–2002》
- ☐ **millionaire** 名 百万長者, 大金持ち
- ☐ **mind** 名 考え
- ☐ **Mini** 名 iPod mini (アイポッド ミニ)《アップル社の携帯型音楽プレイヤー》
- ☐ **minimalist** 名 ミニマリズムの, 必要最低限度の
- ☐ **mirror** 名 鏡
- ☐ **mistake** 熟 make a mistake 間違いをする
- ☐ **mobile phone** 携帯電話
- ☐ **model** 名 ①模型, ひな形 ②型, 形式, モデル
- ☐ **Mona** 名 モナ《実の妹》
- ☐ **money** 熟 save up money 貯金する short of money お金に不自由して
- ☐ **monitor** 名 モニター, (コンピュータ)ディスプレイ
- ☐ **Monsters, Inc.** モンスターズ・インク《ディズニーとピクサー製作のフルCGアニメーション映画, 2001》
- ☐ **more** 熟 not 〜 any more もう[これ以上]〜ない
- ☐ **Moscow** 名 モスクワ《ロシアの首都》
- ☐ **Motorola** 名 モトローラ《アメリカの電子・通信機器メーカー》
- ☐ **mouse** 名 ①(ハツカ)ネズミ ②(コンピュータの)マウス
- ☐ **MP3** 名 MP3(エムピースリー)《音響データを扱うための圧縮技術, またはそれから作られる音声ファイルフォーマット》
- ☐ **multi-touch** 形 マルチタッチ《複数のポイントに同時に触れて操作することができる入力方式》の
- ☐ **multimedia** 名 マルチメディア
- ☐ **musician** 名 音楽家
- ☐ **MusicNet** MusicNet(ミュージックネット)《音楽配信サイト》
- ☐ **Muslim** 名 イスラム教徒, ムスリム 形 イスラム教[文明]の

N

- ☐ **naked** 形 ①裸の, むき出しの ②覆いのない, ありのままの
- ☐ **Nano** 名 iPod nano (アイポッド ナノ)《アップル社の携帯型音楽プレイヤー》
- ☐ **NASDAQ** 略 店頭株式市場, ナスダック《= National Association of Securities Dealers Automated Quotation》

Word List

- **national park** 国立公園
- **nearby** 形 近くの, 間近の 副 近くで, 間近で
- **nearly** 副 ①近くに, 親しく ②ほとんど, あやうく
- **necessary** 形 必要な, 必然の
- **negative** 形 否定的な
- **negotiate** 動 交渉［協議］する
- **neighborhood** 名 近所（の人々）, 付近
- **neither** 副《否定文に続いて》〜も…しない
- **nervous** 形 神経質な, おどおどした
- **netbook** 名 ネットブック《基本的なインターネット上のサービスを利用することを主な用途とした, 安価で小型軽量なノートパソコン》
- **Netherlands** 名 オランダ《国名》
- **New York** ニューヨーク《米国の都市；州》
- **news** 名 報道, ニュース, 便り, 知らせ
- **newspaper** 名 新聞（紙）
- **Newton** 名 Apple Newton ((アップル・ニュートン)《世界初の個人用携帯情報端末（PDA）》
- **NeXT** 名 NeXT, Inc. (ネクスト社)《コンピュータ企業。アップル社を辞めたスティーブ・ジョブズが1985年に創業し, 1996年アップル社に買収される》
- **NeXTSTEP** 名 NeXTSTEP (ネクストステップ)《NeXT社が開発したマルチタスクオペレーティングシステム（OS）》
- **nicely** 副 ①うまく, よく ②上手に, 親切に, 几帳面に
- **no bigger than**《be –》〜ほどの大きさだ
- **no one** 誰も［一人も］〜ない **no one else** 他の誰一人として〜しない
- **noise** 名 騒音, 騒ぎ, 物音
- **Nolan Bushnell** ノーラン・ブッシュネル《アタリ社の創業者, 1943–》
- **nominate** 動 ①指名する, 推薦する ②指定する
- **non-technical** 形 専門家でない一般の
- **none** 代（〜の）何も［誰も・少しも］…ない
- **normal** 形 普通の, 平均の, 標準的な
- **Norman Foster, Sir** ノーマン・フォスター卿《イギリスの建築家, 1935–》
- **not 〜 any more** もう［これ以上］〜ない
- **not 〜 but ...** 〜ではなくて…
- **not matter** 問題にならない
- **notice** 動 気づく
- **novel** 名（長編）小説
- **novelist** 名 小説家
- **now** 熟 **by now** 今のところ, 今ごろまでには

O

- **offer** 動 申し出る, 申し込む, 提供する
- **okay** 形《許可, 同意, 満足などを表して》よろしい, 正しい
- **once in a while** たまに, 時々
- **one another** お互い
- **one day**（過去の）ある日,（未来の）いつか
- **one-player** 形 シングルプレイ用の
- **online** 名 オンライン 形 オンラインの, ネットワーク上の
- **operating system** オペレーティング・システム, 基本ソフト《略称 OS》
- **operation** 名 手術

- **opposite** 名 反対の人[物]
- **orchard** 名 果樹園
- **ordinary** 形 ①普通の, 通常の ②並の, 平凡な **ordinary people** 一般人, 世間一般の人
- **Oregon** 名 オレゴン州《地名》
- **organize** 動 組織する
- **origin** 名 起源, 出自
- **original** 形 始めの, 元の, 本来の
- **originally** 副 元は, 元来
- **OS** 略 オペレーティング・システム, 基本ソフト《operating system の略》
- **out of** **out of the box** 買ったその日から使える **take out of** ～から出す
- **outgoing** 形 ①出て行く, 引退する ②社交的な
- **outsource** 動 (業務を)外注する
- **over** 熟《be –》終わる

P

- **packaging** 名 梱包デザイン, パッケージング
- **paddle** 名 (ピンポンの)ラケット
- **paid** 動 pay (払う)の過去, 過去分詞
- **pair** 名 (2つから成る)一対, 一組, ペア
- **Palo Alto** パロアルト《地名》
- **pancreas** 名 膵臓
- **PARC** 略 パロアルト研究所《カリフォルニア州パロアルトにある研究開発企業. Palo Alto Research Center の略》
- **parent** 名 ①《-s》両親 ②先祖
- **part** 熟 **in part** 一部分において, 一つには
- **partner** 名 仲間, 共同経営者, ビジネス・パートナー
- **pass away** 死ぬ
- **passion** 名 情熱, (～への)熱中, 激怒
- **past** 形 過去の, この前の
- **Patty** 名 パティ《妹(ポールとクララ・ジョブズがスティーブの2年後に養子に迎えた), 1958-》
- **Paul Jobs** ポール・ジョブズ《養父, 1922-1993》
- **Paul Rand** ポール・ランド《アメリカのグラフィックデザイナー, 1914-1996》
- **pay** 支払う, 払う **pay back** 返済する, お返しをする
- **PC** 略 パーソナル・コンピュータ, パソコン《= personal computer》
- **people** 熟 **ordinary people** 一般人, 世間一般の人
- **Pepsi** 名 ペプシ(コーラ)《ソフトドリンク》
- **Pepsi Challenge** 名 ペプシチャレンジ《ペプシコ社の, 比較広告を軸とした広告企画》
- **Pepsi-Cola** 名 ペプシコーラ《ソフトドリンク》
- **PepsiCo** 名 ペプシコ《ペプシコーラで知られる食品・飲料会社》
- **per** 前 ～につき, ～ごとに **per square foot** 1平方フィートあたり
- **perhaps** 副 たぶん, ことによると
- **period** 名 期, 期間, 時代
- **personal** 形 個人の, 私的な
- **personal computer** パーソナル・コンピュータ, パソコン, PC
- **personal digital assistant** 携帯(情報)端末, PDA
- **personality** 名 人格, 個性
- **persuade** 動 説得する, 促して～させる
- **philosophy** 名 哲学, 主義, 信条
- **phone book** 電話帳, 電話番号簿
- **phone phreaker** フリーカー《電

WORD LIST

- photo 名写真 〔話回線に精通するクラッカー。無料で電話回線を使用する人〕
- photo 名写真
- photocopier 名コピー機
- photograph 名写真
- phreaker 名フリーカー《電話回線に精通するクラッカー。無料で電話回線を使用する人》
- picture 熟 take a picture 写真を撮る
- ping-pong 名卓球
- pioneer 名開拓者, 先駆者
- piracy 名著作権侵害
- Pixar 名ピクサー《アメリカの映像制作会社》
- Pixar Image Computer ピクサー・イメージ・コンピュータ《コンピュータグラフィックス製作用の専用コンピュータ》
- plain wood 白木
- plate glass 厚板ガラス
- player 名①競技者, 選手 ②演奏装置
- playful 形ふざけた, 陽気な
- point-and-shoot 形オートフォーカス, 自動露出の
- polite 形ていねいな, 礼儀正しい, 洗練された
- political 形政治の
- Pong 名ポン《アタリ社が1972年に発表したテレビ卓球ゲーム》
- pop 名《-s》ポップス, ポピュラー音楽
- pope 名《the》ローマ教皇
- popular with 《be –》~に人気がある
- pornography 名ポルノ, ポルノグラフィー
- Porsche 名ポルシェ《ドイツの自動車メーカー》
- portable 形持ち運びのできる, ポータブルな
- positive 形積極的な
- possible 形①可能な ②ありうる, 起こりうる as ~ as possible できるだけ~
- practical 形実際的な, 実用的な, 役に立つ
- prank 名(悪意のない)いたずら, 悪ふざけ
- pregnant 形妊娠している
- presentation 名実演, プレゼンテーション
- president 名①大統領 ②社長
- press 名報道機関, マスコミ
- press release プレスリリース, 報道発表
- PressPlay 名PressPlay(プレスプレイ)《音楽配信サイト, 2002–2003》
- pretend 動ふりをする, 装う
- previous 形前の, 先の
- price 名値段
- prime minister 総理大臣, 首相
- princess 名王女
- Princess Diana ダイアナ元英皇太子妃《1961–1997》
- printer 名印刷機, プリンター
- process 名①過程, 経過, 進行 ②手順, 方法, 製法, 加工
- processor 名処理装置, プロセッサー
- procurement 名調達
- product 名製品
- production 名製造, 生産
- professional 形専門の, プロの, 職業的な 名専門家, プロ
- profit 名利益, 利潤, ため
- profit-sharing 形利益分配(制)の
- profitable 形利益になる, 有益な
- progress 動前進する

- □ **project** 名計画, プロジェクト
- □ **promote** 動促進する
- □ **properly** 副適切に, きっちりと
- □ **propose** 動申し込む, 提案する
- □ **prototype** 名試作品
- □ **prove** 動①証明する ②(〜である ことが)わかる, (〜と)なる
- □ **provocative** 形刺激的な, 挑発的
- □ **public** 名一般の人々, 大衆
- □ **publicist** 名パブリシスト, 広報(者)
- □ **publishing** 名出版業
- □ **push out** 押し出す
- □ **put 〜 above …** 〜を…より優先させる
- □ **put up** 〜を上げる, 揚げる, 飾る
- □ **put up someone for adoption** (人)を養子に出す

Q

- □ **quickly** 副敏速に, 急いで
- □ **quit** 動やめる, 辞職する, 中止する

R

- □ **raid** 動急襲する, 手入れする
- □ **Rams, Dieter** ディーター・ラムス《ドイツのインダストリアルデザイナー, 1932-》
- □ **Rand, Paul** ポール・ランド《アメリカのグラフィックデザイナー, 1914-1996》
- □ **rang** 動 ring (鳴る)の過去
- □ **Raskin, Jef** ジェフ・ラスキン《コンピュータ技術者, アップルコンピュータのマッキントッシュの開発を立ち上げた。1943-2005》
- □ **rather** 副①むしろ, かえって ②かなり, いくぶん, やや ③それどころか逆に **rather like** 〜に似ている
- □ **reaction** 名反応, 反動, 反抗, 影響
- □ **ready to** 《be −》すぐに[いつでも]〜できる, 〜する構えで
- □ **realize** 動理解する, 実現する
- □ **rebel** 名反逆者, 反抗者
- □ **rebellious** 形反抗的な, 反逆する
- □ **rebuild** 動再建する, 改造する
- □ **record** 名(音楽などの)レコード 動録音[録画]する
- □ **record company** レコード会社
- □ **redesign** 動再設計する
- □ **Reed** 名リード《ジョブズの息子》
- □ **Reed College** リード大学《オレゴン州にある, 東部のアイビーリーグなどと並ぶ名門大のひとつ》
- □ **refine** 動純化する, 精錬[精製]する, 洗練する
- □ **refuse** 動拒絶する, 断る
- □ **Regis McKenna** レジス・マッケンナ《インテル, アップルなどのハイテク企業をクライアントに持つマーケティングコンサルタント》
- □ **regular** 形①規則的な, 秩序のある ②定期的な, 一定の, 習慣的
- □ **Regular Guy, A** A Regular Guy(レギュラー・ガイ)《小説, 1997》
- □ **regularly** 副整然と, 規則的に
- □ **relationship** 名関係, 関連, 血縁関係
- □ **release** 動発表する, リリースする 名解放, 釈放 **press release** プレスリリース, 報道発表
- □ **religion** 名宗教, 〜教, 信条
- □ **remarkable** 形注目に値する, すばらしい
- □ **remind** 動思い出させる, 気づかせる
- □ **remote** 形(距離・時間的に)遠い, 遠隔の

Word List

- **remove** 動 取り去る, 除去する
- **renaissance** 名（文化や学問などの）復興, 再生
- **render** 動 表現［描写］する, 絵などに表す
- **reorganize** 動 再編成する, 再組織する
- **repair** 動 修理［修繕］する
- **replace** 動 ①取り替える, 差し替える ②元に戻す
- **repo man** 名（支払い滞納が生じた商品の）回収屋
- **research** 名 調査, 研究
- **reserved seat** 指定席, 予約席
- **resign** 動 辞職する, やめる, 断念する
- **respond** 動 答える, 返答［応答］する
- **responsibility** 名 ①責任, 義務, 義理 ②負担, 責務
- **restructure** 動 再編成する, 再構築する
- **result** 名 結果, 成り行き, 成績 **as a result** その結果（として）
- **retailer** 名 小売り業者, 小売り店
- **retire** 動 引き下がる, 退職［引退］する
- **return** 熟 **in return** お返しとして
- **revenue** 名 所得, 収入, 利益
- **revolution** 名 革命, 変革
- **revolutionary** 形 革命の, 画期的な, 革命的な
- **rewind** 動 巻き直す
- **Ridley Scott** リドリー・スコット《イギリス出身の映画監督, 映画プロデューサー, 1937–》
- **risk** 名 危険
- **rival** 名 競争相手, 匹敵する人
- **Robert Friedland** ロバート・フリードランド《Ivanhoe Mines (アイバンホー・マインズ, カナダに本社を置く資源企業) 会長。リード大学在籍時, 彼からジョブズは「人を惹き付ける方法」を学んだ》
- **robot** 名 ロボット
- **rock'n'roll** 名 ロックンロール《音楽》
- **rocker** 名 ロック歌手［シンガー］, ロッカー
- **rocket** 名 ロケット
- **ROKR** 名 ROKR (ロッカー)《モトローラ社の音楽携帯電話, 2005》
- **Rolling Stones** ローリングストーンズ《英国のロックバンド》
- **Rome** 名 ①ローマ《イタリアの首都》②古代ローマ（帝国）
- **Ron Johnson** ロン・ジョンソン《ジョブズにターゲット (Target) から引き抜かれ, Apple Store を約11年間余りでゼロから現在の規模（店舗数300以上, 部門従業員数約3万人）までに育て上げた》
- **Ron Wayne** ロン・ウェイン《アップル社の共同設立者の一人, 1934–》
- **Ross Perot** ロス・ペロー《アメリカの実業家, 政治家, 1930–》
- **row** 名（横に並んだ）列 **in a row** 1列に（並んで）, 連続して
- **royalty** 名 著作権使用料, 印税
- **rude** 形 粗野な, 無作法な, 失礼な
- **rudeness** 名 無礼, 不作法

S

- **sadden** 動 ～を悲しませる
- **sadly** 副 悲しそうに, 不幸にも
- **salary** 名 給料
- **sale** 名 販売, 取引, 大売り出し **go on sale** 発売される, 市場に出回る
- **sales** 形 販売の
- **San Francisco** サンフランシスコ《米国の都市》

- **San Francisco Bay Area** サンフランシスコ湾岸地帯［ベイエリア］
- **San Francisco Symphony Hall** デービス・シンフォニーホール《サンフランシスコ交響楽団の本拠地》
- **save up money** 貯金する
- **scan** 名 スキャン, 精査
- **schedule** 名 予定, スケジュール
- **screen** 名 仕切り, 幕, スクリーン, 画面
- **scroll** 動（コンピュータで）スクロールする
- **Sculley, John** ジョン・スカリー《アメリカ実業家。ペプシコーラ社長とアップルコンピュータの社長, CEO を歴任。1939–》
- **seat** 熟 reserved seat 指定席, 予約席
- **second-largest** 形（規模が）2 番目に大きい
- **secretary of state** 国務長官
- **see-through** 形 シースルーの, 透けて見える
- **seldom** 副 まれに, めったに～ない
- **self-confident** 形 自信のある, 自信過剰の
- **semiconductor** 名 半導体
- **sensation** 名 大評判, センセーション
- **sense** 名 ①感覚, 感じ ②常識, 分別, センス common sense 常識, 共通感覚
- **separate** 動 ①分ける, 分かれる, 隔てる ②別れる, 別れさせる 形 ①分かれた, 別れた, 別々の
- **series** 名 一続き, 連続, シリーズ
- **server** 名 サーバー
- **service** 名 ①勤務, 業務 ②サービス ③宗教的な儀式
- **set up** ①配置する, セットする ②創立する, 設立する
- **shadow** 名 影
- **shape** 名 形, 姿, 型
- **shaped** 形 ～の形をした
- **shareholder** 名 株主
- **shave** 動（ひげ・顔を）そる, 削る
- **shit** 名 くそ, 最低のもの
- **shocked** 形《be ～》ショックを受ける, がくぜんとする
- **short of money** お金に不自由して
- **shown** 動 show（見せる）の過去分詞
- **Shuffle** 名 iPod shuffle（アイポッド シャッフル）《アップル社の携帯型音楽プレイヤー》
- **shy** 形 内気な, 恥ずかしがりの, 臆病な
- **side** 名 側, 横, そば, 斜面
- **silhouette** 名 シルエット, 影絵
- **Silicon Valley** シリコン・バレー《アメリカ合衆国西部のカリフォルニア州にある工業集積地域》
- **silversmith** 銀細工師
- **similar** 形 同じような, 類似した, 相似の
- **simplicity** 名 単純, 質素
- **single** 名 シングル CD（曲）
- **skip** 動（途中を）抜かす, 飛ばす
- **slogan** 名 スローガン, モットー
- **smart** 形 きちんとした, 洗練された
- **smartphone** 名 スマートフォン
- **smash hit** スマッシュヒット, 大ヒット, 大ブレイク
- **smelly** 形 いやなにおいのする
- **smoothly** 副 滑らかに, 流ちょうに
- **so** 熟 and so そこで, それだから, それで so ～ that … 非常に～なの

WORD LIST

- で… so many 非常に多くの
- **software** 名 ソフト(ウェア)
- **solve** 動 解く, 解決する
- **somebody** 代 誰か, ある人
- **somehow** 副 ①どうにかこうにか, ともかく, 何とかして ②どういうわけか
- **someone** 代 ある人, 誰か
- **something** 代 ①ある物, 何か ②いくぶん, 多少
- **Sony** 名 ソニー《日本の大手電子機器・電機メーカー》
- **soon** 熟 as soon as ～するとすぐ, ～するや否や
- **sophisticated** 形 洗練された
- **sophistication** 名 洗練
- **sort** 名 種類, 品質
- **source** 名 源, 原因, もと
- **spaceman** 名 宇宙飛行士
- **spark** 名 ①火花 ②ひらめき, 輝き
- **speaker** 名 スピーカー, 拡声器
- **specialist** 名 専門家, スペシャリスト
- **specialize** 動 専門にする, 専攻する, 特別にする
- **specialized** 動 specialize(専門にする)の過去, 過去分詞 形 専門の, 分化した
- **speech** 熟 make a speech 演説をする
- **speed** 名 速力, 速度 動 急ぐ, 急がせる speed up 速度を上げる, 速める
- **spirit** 名 ①霊 ②精神, 気力
- **split** 名 割ること, 分割
- **spreadsheet** 名 表計算
- **square** 名 ①正方形 ②乗, 平方
- **square foot** 平方フィート per square foot 1平方フィートあたり
- **stack** 動 積み重ねる
- **staff** 名 職員, スタッフ
- **stage** 名 舞台
- **staircase** 名 階段
- **standard** 名 標準, 規格, 規準
- **Stanford University** スタンフォード大学《アメリカの私立大学》
- **Star Wars** スター・ウォーズ《映画》
- **start** 熟 get started 始める
- **state** 名 国家, (アメリカなどの)州
- **steal** 動 盗む
- **steel** 名 鋼, 鋼鉄(製の物)
- **Stephen Wozniak** スティーブ・ウォズニアック《同じ高校の卒業生で, アップル・コンピュータ社の共同創設者》
- **Steve Jobs** スティーブ・ジョブズ《アップル社の共同設立者の一人, 1955–2011》
- **Steven Paul Jobs** スティーブ・ジョブズ《アップル社の共同設立者の一人, 1955–2011》のフルネーム
- **stock** 名 株式
- **stock market** 株式市場
- **stone** 名 石, 小石
- **storage system** ストレージシステム
- **strategy** 名 戦略, 作戦, 方針
- **strong-willed** 形 意志の強い, 断固とした
- **studio** 名 スタジオ, 仕事場
- **style** 名 やり方, 流儀, 様式, スタイル
- **stylish** 形 流行の, スタイリッシュな
- **stylus** 名 スタイラスペン, タッチペン
- **suburb** 名 近郊, 郊外
- **success** 名 成功, 幸運, 上首尾
- **successful** 形 成功した, うまくいった
- **successfully** 副 首尾よく, うまく

113

- **sugared water** 砂糖水
- **suggest** 動 ①提案する ②示唆する
- **suit** 名 スーツ、背広
- **summit** 名 《the –》首脳会議、サミット
- **Super Bowl** スーパーボウル《米プロフットボウルの王座決定戦》
- **supergroup** 名 スーパーグループ《音楽》
- **supermarket** 名 スーパーマーケット
- **supplier** 名 供給者、供給業者、納入業者
- **supply** 名 供給(品)、補充
- **supply chain management** サプライチェーン・マネジメント、供給連鎖管理、SCM
- **support** 動 養う、援助する
- **sure** 熟 make sure 確かめる、確認する
- **surround** 動 囲む、包囲する
- **sweat** 動 汗をかく
- **symbol** 名 シンボル、象徴
- **symphony** 名 交響楽、シンフォニー
- **Syria** 名 シリア《国名》
- **Syrian** 形 シリア人の

T

- **tablet** 名 ①錠剤、タブレット ②便箋、メモ帳 ③銘板
- **tablet PC** タブレット型パソコン
- **tagline** 名 キャッチフレーズ
- **take** 熟 take a bath 風呂に入る take a picture 写真を撮る take advantage of ～を利用する、～につけ込む take back 取り戻す take care 気をつける、注意する take care of ～の世話をする、～面倒を見る、～を管理する take off 離陸する、出発する take out of ～から出す take over 引き継ぐ、支配する、乗っ取る
- **takeover** 名 支配権の取得
- **talented** 形 才能のある、有能な
- **talker** 名 話す人
- **Tangerine** 名 Tangerine (タンジェリン)《ロンドンにあるデザインエージェンシー》
- **Target** 名 ターゲット《アメリカの大手小売企業》
- **teaching assistant** 教育[授業]助手
- **technical** 形 技術(上)の、工業の、専門の
- **technique** 名 テクニック、技術、手法
- **technology** 名 テクノロジー、科学技術
- **teenager** 名 10代の人、ティーンエイジャー《13歳から19歳》
- **telecommunications** 名 電子機器による遠距離通信
- **television** 名 テレビ
- **temple** 名 寺、神殿
- **Tennessee** 名 テネシー州《地名》
- **term of deal** 契約条件
- **Texas** 名 テキサス州《地名》
- **text** 名 テキスト、文字列 text display 文字表示
- **that** 熟 after that その後 so ~ that … 非常に～なので…
- **theme** 名 主題、テーマ
- **then-girlfriend** 名 当時のガールフレンド
- **therapy** 名 治療
- **therefore** 副 したがって、それゆえ、その結果
- **thin** 形 薄い、細い、やせた
- **Think Different** Think Different

Word List

（シンク ディファレント）《アップル社の1997年当時の広告スローガン》

- **those** 熟 **in those days** あのころは, 当時は
- **though** 接 ①～にもかかわらず, ～だが ②たとえ～でも **even though** ～であるけれども, ～にもかかわらず 副 しかし
- **3-D** 形 三次元の, 立体映像の
- **Tim Cook** ティム・クック《アップル社CEO, 1960–》
- **time** 熟 **at the time** そのころ, 当時は **at this time** 現時点では, このとき **by the time** ～する時までに **for the first time** 初めて
- **timid** 形 気の小さい, 臆病な, おどおどした
- **Tin Toy** 『ティン・トイ』《短編CGアニメーション。アカデミー賞短編アニメ賞受賞, 1988》
- **tip** 名 チップ, 心づけ
- **tired** 形 疲れた, くたびれた
- **titanium** 名 チタン
- **title** 名 肩書 **job title** 仕事の肩書, 職位
- **ton** 名 ①トン《重量・容量単位》②《-s》たくさん
- **too** 熟 **far too** あまりにも～過ぎる
- **tool** 名 道具, 用具, 工具
- **Toshiba** 東芝《大手家電, 電子, 電気機器製造メーカー》
- **total** 名 全体, 合計
- **totalitarian state** 全体主義国家
- **touch control** タッチ操作
- **touchscreen** 名 タッチスクリーン, タッチパネル
- **tough** 形 堅い, 丈夫で, たくましい, 骨の折れる, 困難な
- **Toy Story** 『トイ・ストーリー』《アニメーション映画, 1995》
- **Toy Story 2** 『トイ・ストーリー2』《アニメーション映画, 1999》
- **traditional** 形 伝統的な
- **transfer** 動 ①移動する ②移す ③譲渡する
- **transplant** 名 移植
- **trap** 動 わなを仕掛ける, わなで捕らえる
- **treatment** 名 治療（法）
- **trick** 名 策略
- **Trinitron** 名 トリニトロン《ソニーが開発したブラウン管》
- **trouble** 熟 **in trouble** 面倒な状況で, 困って
- **truly** 副 本当に, 真に
- **tumor** 名 腫瘍
- **turn of events** 出来事の節目
- **turn out** ～と判明する, （結局～に）なる
- **Twitter** 名 ツイッター《米国Twitter社によるミニブログサービス》
- **typical** 形 典型的な, 象徴的な

U

- **U.S. secretary of state** 米国務長官
- **U2** 名 U2（ユーツー）《アイルランド出身のロックバンド》
- **ugly** 形 ①醜い, ぶかっこうな ②いやな, 不快な
- **ultimate** 形 究極の
- **underneath** 副 下に［を］, 根底は
- **unique** 形 唯一の, ユニークな, 独自の
- **unit** 名 ユニット, 構成単位, 1個
- **United States** 名 アメリカ合衆国《国名》
- **Universal** 名 ユニバーサル（ミュージック・グループ）《アメリカのレコード会社》

- □ **university** 名(総合)大学
- □ **University of Delaware** デラウェア大学
- □ **University of Wisconcin** ウィスコンシン大学
- □ **unlike** 形似ていない、違った 前〜と違って
- □ **unusual** 形普通でない、珍しい、見[聞き]慣れない
- □ **unveil** 動ベールを取る、明らかにする
- □ **up to** 〜まで、〜に至るまで **go up to** 〜まで行く、近づく
- □ **used to** 助①以前は〜だった、以前はよく〜したものだった ②《be-》〜に慣れる
- □ **user** 名使用者、利用者、消費者
- □ **usual** 形通常の、いつもの、平常の、普通の **as usual** いつものように、相変わらず

V

- □ **valley** 名谷、谷間
- □ **valuable** 形貴重な、価値のある、役に立つ
- □ **variety** 名①変化、多様性、寄せ集め ②種類
- □ **various** 形変化に富んだ、さまざまの、たくさんの
- □ **Vatican** 名ローマ法王
- □ **ve** 代weのドイツ語訛り風発音
- □ **vegetable** 名野菜、青物
- □ **vegetarian** 形菜食主義の
- □ **vegetarianism** 名菜食主義
- □ **version** 名バージョン、版
- □ **Vertigo** 名「ヴァーティゴ」《U2のシングル曲、2004》
- □ **video game** テレビ[ビデオ]・ゲーム
- □ **Virginia** 名バージニア州《地名》
- □ **VisiCalc** 名 VisiCalc(ビジカルク)《世界初のパーソナルコンピュータ向け表計算ソフトウエア、1979》
- □ **vision** 名先見、洞察力
- □ **visionary** 形先見の明のある、ビジョンを持った人
- □ **visitor** 名訪問客
- □ **Volkswagen** 名フォルクスワーゲン《ドイツの自動車メーカー》

W

- □ **waiting list** 順番待ちリスト
- □ **warehouse** 名倉庫、問屋、商品保管所
- □ **Warner** 名(タイム・)ワーナー《アメリカの総合メディア企業》
- □ **Washington, D.C.** ワシントンD.C.《地名》
- □ **Wayne, Ron** ロン・ウェイン《アップル社の共同設立者の一人、1934-》
- □ **website** 名ウェブサイト、ホームページ
- □ **wedding** 名結婚式、婚礼
- □ **well** 熟 **as well as** 〜と同様に **do well** 成績が良い、成功する **get on well** うまくやっていく、肌が合う
- □ **well-designed** 副うまく設計された
- □ **West Coast Computer Faire** ウェストコースト・コンピュータフェア《サンフランシスコで開催、1977年4月16日の第一回がApple IIお披露目の会場となった》
- □ **Westinghouse** 名ウェスティングハウス(・エレクトリック)《アメリカの総合電機メーカー》
- □ **What about 〜?** 〜についてあなたはどう思いますか。〜はどうですか。

Word List

- **whatever** 代 ①《関係代名詞》〜するものは何でも ②どんなこと[もの]が〜とも 形 ①どんな〜でも ②《否定文・疑問文で》少しの〜も, 何らかの
- **wheel** 名 輪, 車輪 Click Wheel クリックホイール《iPodシリーズに搭載されている操作インタフェース。ドーナツ状のタッチパッドの中心に円形のボタンが配置され片手で様々な操作が可能》
- **whenever** 接 ①〜するときはいつでも, 〜するたびに ②いつ〜しても
- **while** 熟 once in a while たまに, 時々
- **whole** 形 全体の, すべての, 完全な 名《the-》全体, 全部 as a whole 全体として
- **whom** 代 ①誰を[に] ②《関係代名詞》〜するところの人, そしてその人を
- **wicked** 形 悪い, 不道徳な
- **widescreen** 形 ワイドスクリーンの, 画面の広い
- **Windows** 名 (マイクロソフト・)ウィンドウズ《マイクロソフトのオペレーティング システムのシリーズ》
- **winner** 名 勝利者, 成功者
- **wire** 名 電線
- **wise** 形 賢明な, 聡明な, 博学の
- **within** 前 ①〜の中[内]に, 〜の内部に ②〜以内で, 〜を越えないで
- **woke** 動 wake (目が覚める) の過去
- **Woody** 名 ウッディ《アニメーション映画『Toy Story』の登場人物》
- **Word** 名 (マイクロソフト・)ワード《Microsoft Word. 文書作成ソフトウェア》
- **work on** 〜で働く, 〜に取り組む, 〜を説得する, 〜に効く
- **workbench** 名 作業台
- **worker** 名 仕事をする人, 労働者
- **worldwide** 形 世界的な, 世界中に広まった, 世界規模の 副 世界中に[で], 世界的に
- **Worldwide Developers Conference** ワールドワイド・デベロッパーズ・カンファレンス《アップル社が毎年開催している開発者向けイベント》
- **worried** 動 worry (悩む) の過去, 過去分詞 be worried about (〜のことで) 心配している, 〜が気になる[かかる] 形 心配そうな, 不安げな
- **worse** 形 いっそう悪い, より劣った, よりひどい 副 いっそう悪く get worse 悪化する
- **worth** 形 (〜の) 価値がある, (〜) しがいがある 名 価値, 値打ち
- **would have ... if 〜** もし〜だったとしたら…しただろう《仮定法》
- **Wozniak, Stephen** スティーブ・ウォズニアック《同じ高校の卒業生で, アップル・コンピュータ社の共同創設者》

X・Y・Z

- **Xerox** 名 ゼロックス《アメリカの印刷機器の製造販売会社》
- **Xerox Palo Alto Research Center** パロアルト研究所《カリフォルニア州パロアルトにある研究開発企業, 略称PARC》
- **Yosemite National Park** ヨセミテ国立公園
- **Zen Buddhism** 禅 (宗)

E-CAT

English **C**onversational **A**bility **T**est
国際英語会話能力検定

● E-CATとは…
英語が話せるようになるためのテストです。インターネットベースで、30分であなたの発話力をチェックします。

www.ecatexam.com

iTEP

● iTEP®とは…
世界各国の企業、政府機関、アメリカの大学300校以上が、英語能力判定テストとして採用。オンラインによる90分のテストで文法、リーディング、リスニング、ライティング、スピーキングの5技能をスコア化。iTEP®は、留学、就職、海外赴任などに必要な、世界に通用する英語力を総合的に評価する画期的なテストです。

www.itepexamjapan.com

ラダーシリーズ
The Steve Jobs Story スティーブ・ジョブズ・ストーリー

2012年2月2日 第1刷発行
2024年8月8日 第18刷発行

著者　トム・クリスティアン

発行者　賀川 洋

発行所　IBCパブリッシング株式会社
〒162-0804 東京都新宿区中里町29番3号
菱秀神楽坂ビル
Tel. 03-3513-4511　Fax. 03-3513-4512
www.ibcpub.co.jp

© IBC Publishing, Inc. 2012

印刷　株式会社シナノパブリッシングプレス
装丁　伊藤 理恵
組版データ　ITC Giovanni Std Book + Frutiger 65 Bold

落丁本・乱丁本は、小社宛にお送りください。送料小社負担にてお取り替えいたします。本書の無断複写（コピー）は著作権法上での例外を除き禁じられています。

Printed in Japan
ISBN978-4-7946-0123-0